Invading the Indigenous while the Rest of Us Watch

Douglas H. Melloy

If you purchased this book without a cover you should be aware that this book is stolen property. It was reported as 'unsold and destroyed" to the Publisher and neither the Author nor the Publisher has received any payment for this "stripped book.

Copyright ©2023 Douglas H. Melloy

All rights reserved. No part of this book may be used or reproduced by any means, graphic, electronic, or mechanical, including photocopying, recording, taping or by any information storage retrieval system without the written permission of the publisher except in the case of brief quotations embodied in critical articles and reviews.

Because of the dynamic nature of the Internet, any web addresses or links contained in this book may have changed since publication and may no longer be valid. The views expressed in this work are solely those of the author and do not necessarily reflect the views of the publisher, and the publisher hereby disclaims any responsibility for them.

Paperback:ISBN 979-8-9882586-5-0

LCCN: Filed and pending.

Published by QuadsmediaFirm
www.quadsmediafirm.com

All materials used for this book was from the Author.

Contents

Dedication 1
Introduction 3

Part 1 7
  The Invader Culture Mindset 7

    In the Beginning 9
    Where Are We Now: 14
    Maintaining the Invader Culture: 29
    Humanity and the Invader Culture: 45
    Invader Culture and the True Nature
    and Purpose of Humanity: 59
    Negativity and Our True Identity 71
    What the Invader Culture Does Not Tell You 77

Part II: 90
  The Indigenous Way of Life 90

    Original Design 91
    Indigenous Ideology 101
    Returning 111

Part III: 114
  The rest of us 114

    Arbitrariness: 115
    God 122
    What the Rest of Us Just Don't 'Get' 129

Part IV: **136**
  Path as Purpose **136**

   The Ego 137
   Evolution, Negativity, and Balance 151
   Ascension 159
   Conclusion 172
   Aware Talk Radio 176

Invading the Indigenous while the Rest of Us Watch

Dedication

This book is humbly, lovingly, and sincerely dedicated to my Chinese father, Professor Chu, Chen-hua. His love and wisdom have mentored me and inspired me to be my best. I am truly grateful he has been my friend, and I appreciate all he has contributed to my life. It is truly an honor for me that he has been a dad for me. His love for me is beyond measure. A great soul, whom I love. thank you ever so much!

This book is also lovingly dedicated to my mother, Elaine B. Melloy; to my two sisters, Diana Emler and Deborah Melloy; to my best friend, Carol Bradshaw; to my other mentor in life, Marge Zachary; to my movie buddy, Bonnie Goodman; to my last girlfriend, Margie Hudson; and to all those people who have impacted my life in those ways needed for me to heal, evolve, and smile.

In loving memory of my brother, David Charles Melloy, and of my father, Robert Charles Melloy. May your lives now be the blessing to us all.

Introduction

I have pondered the idea of the end of the world from a very young age. Many voices are telling us all kinds of ideas as to what is going to happen and why. There are those experts who feel they know. Sources range from Nostradamous; to the book of Revelation; to Ramtha, Mary Summer Rain, Edgar Cayce, and a host of others. There is the Mayan Calendar, with its end date of 2012. Many feel the entire notion of the end of the world is just another Y2K, which proved to be nothing but a multi-billion dollar hoax! We each are left to our imagination about the so-called coming apocalypse. The question I asked myself many years ago was: What aspect of humanity necessitates the need for ending here?

As a child growing up, I watched a lot of westerns about cowboys and Native Americans. Curiously, I always rooted for the Native Americans. I developed an interest in their way of life. I also was curious as to why they existed as they do. As I matured and went to school, education taught me all about world history and how it is based upon wars fought between nations and upon those individuals whose sole purpose in life was engaging in battle.

When one reads the Old Testament, it is a written document informing us of the arrival of the warlord god Jehovah. Jehovah takes possession of his chosen people through covenant that stipulates that, in order to be His chosen, they must annihilate everyone else. Thus began the invader culture mindset on this planet-around 9,000 BC. The psychology of the invader culture mindset is hierarchy, elitism, superiority, chosen-ness, and good versus evil, leading to the social practices of conquering, enslaving, and destroying people, places, and things. This self-serving ideology has not changed since it was introduced to us eleven thousand years ago. War, greed, and class distinction are the invader culture mindset emanating from fear, judgment, and persecution.

The irony of this is, Jesus taught love, forgiveness, and doing unto others to end militarization, money as a form of exchange, and the fiction that one group of people are chosen by God as Its own. Love, forgiveness, and doing unto others also heal fear, judgment, and persecution. When examining the Bible, it can be broken down into three points of view. The Old Testament is negative, while the life of Jesus is positive, and the theology of Paul is arbitrary. Personal and social evolution evolves in the same manner. Each person living on this planet does so according to the negative, positive, or arbitrary as hiser life. We each choose what we wish our life to be as a personal representation. Then we look for what reinforces and supports our chosen points of view.

Humanness evolves according to what is negative, positive, or arbitrary. This is demonstrated through the invader culture mindset, the indigenous way of life, and the rest of humanity. We all get to see firsthand how these operate personally, relationally, socially, globally, and universally. People go about their business not knowing much of anything about what's involved and why. We do not question authority. We blindly follow the agendas of others regardless of what they entail. Blind obedience is rewarded for the faithful by the promise that life after death is heaven. Never mind that the "dead bury the dead; God is only of the living!" The irony of this is that nothing changes humanly, at least not in the last eleven thousand years. Humanity was given two thousand years to incorporate love, forgiveness, and doing unto others, or to face the book of Revelation as its consequence for refusing to return to living as designed. Humanity has refused to do, by keeping militarization, money, and arrogance in tact.

The invader culture mindset will soon become extinct--in the same manner the dinosaurs did millions of years ago. Humanity will return to living as designed, which is the indigenous way of being. For those who live arbitrarily, it is time for you to go home. Home is where your soul comes from. This book explains why the

Invading the Indigenous while the Rest of Us Watch

end of the world is a truth we will all experience. It is the ending of war, greed, and class distinction. It is an ending to the influences that contributed to this planet that are self-serving in nature and intent. According to Ramtha and a few other sources, the warlord god Jehovah returns for His chosen people, who, after being conquered through covenant, and enslaved to a self-serving ideology, are then destroyed when It returns to fulfill this promise. The timeline for this is the end of 2012. This book posits the ideas that the invader culture mindset will become extinct and why, that humanity will return to living its design by becoming the indigenous again, and that those who are living arbitrarily will leave by going home. This will happen within the next three years, by the end of 2012.

Part 1

The Invader Culture Mindset

In the Beginning

Historical social evolution evolves along three courses of development humanly. They are invader cultures, the indigenous, and the rest of humanity. Invader cultures live according to a specific agenda or ideology. The indigenous live according to a specific design. The rest of humanity lives according to the blueprint of the soul.

What defines the invader culture is its emphasis upon militarization-the necessity for war; economics based upon monetary exchange; class distinction; gender disparity; social divisiveness; and social impoverishment. These institutions exemplify every invader culture existing on this planet today. They have remained in place ever since the ideologies were introduced to this planet through covenanted insistence. People are easily fooled and duped into perpetuating what only becomes extinct. Extinction is only possible with people when that which is untenable continues to be their way of life millennia after millennia. Eventually, existence gets on with the process of evolution by separating the wheat from the chaff. Most of humanity will experience this as the end of the reincarnation process, experienced as the end of the world. Eventually, the invader culture and all it entails self-destructs. It destroys itself.

The invader culture mindset begins through the process of a select group of people being conquered through an ideology implemented as an institution that, over time, becomes tradition, like science or religion. Today, the invader culture utilizes the seven institutions of science, religion, education, business, politics, law, and medicine to insure that it remains intact until the end of days. These enslave humanity. Ultimately, what has conquered through ideology and enslaved through tradition causes the destruction of humanity when the time of polarization has ended. For humanity, this may be by the end of the year 2012.

Evolution is the development of consciousness through experience and intention. It requires honest self-reflection. This pondering of the events composing one's life centers on examining both what takes place and the purpose that it serves one's existence. When this is grasped, one will heal, as the catalyst is no longer needed to assist one in moving on and becoming more conscious.

Consciousness is the awareness that one exists as something. It is also the realization that alternative states exist. True enlightenment is when one realizes that he or she is the oneness of everything-that perfection alone is. Perfection is the existence of an ideal, not an ideal that never evolves. This can be thought of as the unified field theory pertaining to one's life.

This is impossible to realize when an individual or culture lives according to the invader mindset, with its insistence that conflict is the way it is, through the belief in good versus evil. When studied, conflict is only possible through hatred. There is no such thing as good hatred and evil hatred. Hatred is the nihilistic attitude one has about him or herself that is projected onto another-usually of the same racial stock or base, like Jew and Arab. The need for hatred is insured through religious and political ideas. These maintain and ensure that nothing changes within the invader culture. Religiously, this belief is martyred through the insane notion of the holy war. Supposedly, God has decided that some human elements are an abomination to It and need to be destroyed, not by God, but through the hands of people. God as love makes the concept of abomination impossible from the perspective of God. Also impossible is the nonsense that God is jealous of people worshipping idols through faith. People make the same mistake now about what comes and why. Christians today believe that Jesus/God returns to pass judgment upon everyone. This is called the 'Day of Judgment.' This was also what the Jews believed about their messiah, that what was coming to them as their 'savior' was someone who was going to judge and destroy the wicked. However, God as love does not destroy or judge,

God loves, heals, and leads people back to living as His image and likeness. Plus the return of God only takes place within the heart, where God resides.

Where did the invader culture come from? Look no further than the Old Testament and its Lord God Jehovah. Why does Lord precede God? Because the Lord God Jehovah is actually the warlord god Jehovah, who took possession of the Jews, representing humanity, as His chosen people through covenanted ideology. This conquered them, enslaved them, and culminates in this culture's destruction when Jehovah returns for His chosen in December of 2012. This is the legacy of His promise, made for keeping and maintaining the faith until this point in time. Jesus came to teach the Jews proper social behavior and ending their relationship to what now returns to destroy them.

According to the Seth Material: "Retention of the Star of David and re-creation of the State of Israel necessitates the return of Jehovah for His people." According to Ramtha, "The last great battle fought will be in the heavens between Jehovah, the Lord God of the Jews, and Id, the bestower of man. By bestower, I mean, that which brought humanness to life, after Yahweh created it. This battle will last seven days, not seven years. The great lights of Jehovah and Id will "light the void" and disrupt the surface of this planet. The life and teachings of Jesus was intended to prevent this, by the Jews choosing to live what he taught while living. The Jews are now faced with the outcome for refusing to recognize and convert to love, forgiveness, and doing unto others. The failure of the Jews to see that Jesus was their messiah culminates in their destruction by the 'god' that they worship as "the one true God." Many will perish due to unresolved fear. Many will leave convinced the world has been destroyed by 'God.' The Lord God Jehovah is to the universe what Hitler was to Germany.

Does this mean I am anti-Semitic? Absolutely not! Why? Because I do not have any negative attitudes about people and the life they choose to experience. Everyone is entitled to hiser life and all it entails. Individually, we are not defined by ideologies, beliefs, or dogmas instituted as tradition. It is the theology/ideology of Judaism (as well as that of several other religions) that now perpetuates the invader culture established by the warlord god Jehovah. The ideology of Jehovah is worshipped as the Judaic faith of those who practice Judaism. Christians also worship the warlord god Jehovah. These are the medium by which the warlord god Jehovah will return.

Life, according to third density, requires understanding how energy works as both positive and negative, existing as the neutral that polarizes into either the right or left hands of God. This also is called self-service or serving others. Some refer to this as either positive or negative polarization. This is why it is important for people to take responsibility and own love and light as hiser embodied spirituality here. What loves does is accept, and what light does is remain even-minded about people, places, and things. Conflict is only possible when people react to someone or something through refusing to resolve what is reacted to as an aspect of one's life. This is why we are told: "What you resist persists."

Many are resistant to being the humanity they are representing by insisting that outer-based ideals are the way it is, as does the invader culture, with its emphasis on hierarchy, elitism, superiority, chosen-ness, and the belief of good versus evil. These are made possible through our holding to fear, judgment, and persecution. Never mind that Jesus taught love, forgiveness, and doing unto others to resolve the entire culture and historicity of those who thrive on invading others! Now, we are faced with our own doom.

Roughly forty-nine million will remain to continue human evolution until it collectively ascends. This means 99.3 percent fail to make the grade. Why? Choosing to be fear rather than love, to judge rather than forgive, to be selfish rather than giving, all for the sake of what--going to heaven? Rewards and punishments only work with those who are not living their life as intended. This is referred to as either martyrdom or personal sacrifice through living according to the dictates of others, rather than being what is real, knowing what is true, and then sharing these with others, humbly and transparently. Rather curious, what people do for the sake of conformity and being accepted by others. To such an extent, the point is missed entirely about why we are here and what we need to accomplish to live a life well lived. It is only what benefits humanity as a whole, not just the chosen or select few.

Where Are We Now:

The Carrot and the Stick; Karma; Service Polarity; The Seven Institutions; Collective Consciousness; the Ego; Choice

What do we emphasize? What do we feel is important to us? This differs for each of us. The irony of individuality is that most of humanity conforms itself to traditional ways of being. Roughly five and a half billion people practice four religions. They are Hinduism, Buddhism, Christianity, and Islam. Infinity invalidates any two people living or existing in the same manner and way. Uniqueness prevents existence living the same experience. It is truly an oxymoron when two people subscribe to the same points of view. It is also a form of insanity. Yet, the majority of people dying today agree that a particular point of view is correct and never allow themselves to move beyond the conjectures posited by some as the way it is under the guise of science, religion, education, business, politics, law, and medicine. These are the traditions of the invader culture mindset. They keep it intact and unchanged. It is why they exist as they do and the purpose they serve. It is the ego that only looks to getting from external sources through what it feels as lack, need, want and wound, and people experience as distraction, dysfunction, and addiction. It is the ego we are here to heal.

Ah, but that is the art of propaganda institutionalized as tradition and expectancy, coupled with blind obedience. We are

Invading the Indigenous while the Rest of Us Watch

expected to follow the rules of ideology to the grave under the premise we will be rewarded for doing so in a state/place that is completely different from where we find ourselves. This is insanity, folks, due to the fact that reality is self-defined as a personal truth that has a direct correspondence to what we experience and evolve into. Reincarnation means we did not get it! The Bible tells us, "As above, so below." It is impossible for people to experience what they are unconscious of, and the un-conceived of remains a potential only. Due to the art of the stick and carrot, few evolve beyond or away from this, humanly. The ego holds the stick tied to ideologies that carrot most of humanity to the grave. This is due to the ego always looking to get from someone or something what it feels it is lacking and in need of externally.

Here in the West, we ignore karma completely, so we go about our business oblivious to all the consequences our actions have as future paybacks, for which we have to atone. Every action we perform has a consequence of application. Intention is anything that affects the life of another in any way. We are responsible for any/all consequences affecting the lives of others and this planet. We get away with nothing. Every emotion, thought, and action accumulates karma. This is why love and wisdom are so essential as our way of life. This way of being requires honesty and humility for success-no hidden agendas.

Outer-based sources lead us all astray. They are the carrots that lemming the ego into crucifying the body unto death for what is only propaganda---to see what one will believe to the death. Ah, the irony of information that confuses, confounds, and destroys us. Traditions ensure we all die and leave never having lived a day in our life!

Nowhere is this more apparent than in the invader culture mindset, with its insistence that war, greed, and class distinction are God's way of existence, through the use of fear, judgment, and persecution. Even after we were told to love, forgive, and do unto others, we have refused to accept these as our ways of being, knowing, and sharing. The lure of violence, animosity, and arrogance are too strong to heal. The golden calfing of the ego seduces many into accepting the invader culture lifestyle. Our comfort and indifference numbs and blinds us to the arrogance of war, greed, and class distinction. War culminates into demise and the end of the world. Greed establishes poverty and destitution. Class distinction results in the fiction of greater and lesser and the figment of gender disparity. These are their legacy and karma. People remain ignorant about what is going on and why.

Blindly, humanity forges on, oblivious to the karma of its invading ways. History reincarnates the insanity of the invader culture mindset. Every great nation living war and greed meets its doom eventually. America is next. War and greed are cancers killing humanity. Health is a state of mind. Disease is a state of mind. This is demonstrated by how invading cultures brought to the indigenous many types of diseases that almost exterminated entire tribes of these people. The indigenous lived a life that was healthy and disease free. The body is a state of mind to which the ego gives a face so that we can see ourselves clearly. I find it fascinating that I never see my own face, only the faces of others. Why? I am you and you are me, and this is why we meet and observe each other. I am reminded here, that, "I only recognize in others what I am guilty of myself." It is only through others that I recognize who I am, for there is only one us of here, and each of us is that one.

Yet, the invader culture way of life exists principally to keep us at odds with each other and our own humanity. Humanity is an abomination and is not allowed to exist. Humanness is despised, and the invader culture mindset converts people into puppets, robots, and zombies. War begins as a video game that becomes three-dimensional when the children come of age. One must ask him or herself, why is war acceptable to any of us? Look no farther than science and religion.

Science denies the existence of God, while religion teaches us false doctrines about God. No one questions this absurdity. Science also uses its 'wisdom' to create weapons of mass destruction under the guise of peace. Nuclear bombs are created to 'ensure' the peace.

Invading the Indigenous while the Rest of Us Watch

They are so deadly that no one would dare to use them. Insanity confuses itself by this kind of nonsense. All one has to do is ask hiser intuition why asteroids exist. The answer is: they are the remnants of planets destroyed by weapons of mass destruction used by selfish souls under the premise of peace and enjoying the good life.

Conquering, enslaving, and then self-destructing are the ways of the invader culture, with its perpetrations of war, greed, and class distinction. I am always fascinated when I meet people who want to end poverty, yet never mention ending greed. Poverty is the flip side of greed. As long as greed remains unchanged, poverty will flourish, due to people thinking they are superior to others. In a medium that is infinite, nothing has greater value than anything else. A grain of sand has as much value/relevance as the planet, solar system, and galaxy. Also, meaning, value, function, and purpose are ours to define and make. I have learned that I give to anything the only meaning and value that it has, as an aspect of my sense of being.

The only aspect of being the invader culture identifies with and relates to is the ego. The ego allows what is infinite a sense of being specific. The ego is the body's awareness that it is something specific, an identity, and engaged. The golden calfing of the ego is idolization and glorification of one's sense of identity through talents professionalized. These are considered false gods by the fallen. The fallen are everyone who dies. Death and disease are necessary for the invader culture to have any success and for making sure nothing changes involving and regarding what comprises the invader culture. Taking possession of and getting from are the ways of the invader and the ego. Living as designed requires owning and giving life to what one is in possession of that is shared with others humbly and transparently.

The way of the invader culture is modern civilization, with its emphasis on nation state, race superiority, gender disparity, militarization, money as economics, and an elitist class governed by the institutions of the invader culture. It is very possible every city and town on this planet now is a version of Sodom and Gomorrah. These are the components ensuring the survival of the invader culture mindset and the return of the warlord god Jehovah to this planet. According to Ramtha, Jehovah is on His way. I am convinced He will arrive within the next three years to finish what began long ago.

* * * * * * *

The warlord god Jehovah came to this planet around 9,000 BC. This warring entity selected as Its chosen people the Jews. This began the legacy of the invader culture as it is practiced today by every 'civilized' nation. The covenant that was established converted a peaceful people into one required to take possession of the land upon which others lived. Conquering involves the adaptation of an ideology that converts a people into perpetrating an ideology that is foreign and contrary to their true/basic natures. This became warring against the indigenous and the image and likeness of God. This is true of any ideology that one decides to believe in as hiser way of being and life. Any ideology that one believes in that is not one's own reality/truth is what has conquered and enslaved the individual and what culminates in destroying the individual as hiser death experience. This is the role the ego plays for us. It is drawn to external sources thinking it is getting something from that source. The ego is the stick and externals are the carrot that lead one to figments of the imagination duped by ideas that are only intended to lead one to the grave after suffering.

The only voice one can rely on for wisdom is intuition. Education has us believing otherwise. We are taken seriously only when we have adopted to ideas of others as our own. Why? This way, we never know and own our own reality/truth. We will never question the fictions others choose to die for and through. Outer-based ideas are only forms of propaganda meant to see what we will believe in strongly enough. The exception is when the ideas shared assist us in our evolution and ascension. The ego is our 'outer' sense of self.

The irony of the invader culture is that it seeks for one end only--the destruction of God, life, and humanness. Death and dying and the perpetuation of war are the measures of success for this way of life, until the end of human development. This is due to not healing conflict within. Then, That which brought to us this way of dying returns to finish what It started long ago. This will be the experience of the end of the world for all those who do not survive this battle of Armageddon. Anyone who is involved psychologically with science, religion, education, business, politics, law, and medicine will succumb to Jehovah's intention of destroying God, life, and human being-ness. The way to escape this is by choosing to return to living as designed, which is living indigenously. The indigenous way of life is how we were created to live humanly. Invader cultures live according to false doctrine. The rest of us observe these two ways of life, not knowing the actual circumstances involving both cultures. Ignorance is bliss.

Most people do not realize that service polarity is the only aspect of humanness that evolves. Both positive and negative service polarity evolves. People live divided, so they do not realize that negativity is as much a path as the positive. Positive and negative energy exists as a neutral state and, also, as a biased state that we observe as male and female, or the masculine and feminine. As it corresponds to us, energy is balanced and biased. We have the opportunity, responsibility, and option of choosing to polarize into someone that serves, either hiser ego or others. This requires of the chooser an understanding of how energy is and works as the positive, the negative, and the neutral. Hence, the role that experiences play. Lacking this service polarity is impossible. This can be thought of as selfishness or selflessness.

Those who live according to the negative path demand that others only do their bidding through blind obedience. This way of service is very prevalent in the military, business, and politics.

Douglas H. Melloy

There are also family dynamics existing in the same manner. Many marriages thrive on catering to the whims of the selfish. It is only the ego that feels it needs to be worshipped and blindly obeyed to the death. The ego then denies this about itself. It then does the insane, it projects itself into an objectification that it then worships and obeys under the pretense that what it is worshipping is 'God.'

The invader culture thrives through the belief of opposites in conflict, from the dogma of good versus evil. That and the conviction of being God's chosen. Every person who has lived and is living is the image and likeness of God as hiser humanity. Only those enslaved hold to the fiction that they are God's chosen people. God does not play favorites with people. Of the hundreds of religions practiced today, is there really any one that is truest? No! Religion is the ego denied and converted into a false god through projection, objectification, and absolutism. So is science.

Anyone or any group that holds to the insanity that they are favored by God, as Its chosen people, and all others condemned, only shows delusion and self-righteous arrogance. God is a choice made by the individual to become that, humanly, through consciously entering into "God centered within heart," thereby converting one's life to this state of being. This is the Immaculate Conception, as it is only done alone and only through consciousness entering into God's state of being centered within the heart.

"Taking possession of" is the way of the invader culture. "Being in possession of" is the life of God's image shared through the path of service as one's purpose. Those who live the invader culture create empires and live as kings or queens. They amass as much as possible, then die, after convincing people their way of life is worthy of all the attention and fortune attained. Denial is the ego's way ensuring that the body will die and one will go to heaven. Heaven and hell are the states of the positive and the negative according to the ego, which does not exist, so they are fictions of the mind according to unresolved fear and ignorance existing as arrogance.

These two points of view are essential for the invader culture mindset to thrive. Throw in some guilt, and success is guaranteed.

Invading the Indigenous while the Rest of Us Watch

Religions thrive on fear, ignorance, and guilt. Especially Christianity. Science and religion have caused more death and destruction than all other causes combined. The warlord god Jehovah's true faithful and chosen are those who live according to science and religion when based and engaged in conflict, war, greed, oppression, and arrogance. True also of those who educate, engage in politics, business, law, and medicine. The outer is what we contribute to, from God, through our life, to others, and the environment. These determine the measure by which we stand or fall.

* * * * * * *

According to Elizabeth Claire Profit and Dannion Brinkley, every one of us goes through a whole life review after passing on. Each of us is shown every emotion, thought, and action, and the effects of them upon others and this planet. Then our life is assessed. We then have to reincarnate to atone for everything negative we perpetrated on others. We return as victims to everything we perpetrated. This is why it is so very important to always be kind and do unto others what enhances their life, as it also enhances our own.

Buddha taught: "Do not do unto others what you do not want done unto you." Jesus taught: "Do unto others as you would have them do unto you." I teach: "You only do unto others what you do unto yourself." Karma teaches us that perpetrator and victim are one person. They mirror like-mindedness. Victims of today are perpetrators of the past. Balancing karma requires reincarnation. People experience firsthand what they perpetrated on another or others. The games of the ego only last for so long. People get away with absolutely nothing humanly. All actions are recorded within the soul and then assessed, and healing gets to take place through karma and reincarnation.

We are each other. Doing unto others, through what we feel and think, only affects us by our own hand. Because there is only oneness and perfection and the technique of extension and expansion, coupled with infinity, which gives us our sense of time's duration and space's placement, so that experience expresses who we are as our humanity. This is energy given our human face. What ideal do we aspire to and stand for humanly? God only knows!

Value and meaning are determined by us, as are ethics, integrity, and morality. Who decides what these are? The responsibility is strictly our own. We are a human definition of God, universe, and this planet. We exist according to the love of Yahweh and the light of Id, as well as through the issues and talents of our biological parents. Coupled with this is the blueprint of our soul. We are responsible for what we are conscious of about all these aspects of being, making us the human we are living. The art of being requires each person to heal issues and develop talents into what is socially and environmentally conducive. Not easy to accomplish because so many people refuse to apply themselves to their own psychology.

Coupled with this are those who deny and reject the notion that anything needs to be done as, and according to, one's life. It's business as usual for those who thrive on all things negative. The point, then, is missed about personal and social evolution. Many only want to work on the top floor. Many ask one question: "Is my ego big enough to win?" Game players make up rules few understand. Those who do become very successful, and many a misguided soul aspires to become just like them under the premise: this is the good life.

The irony of this way of living is it excludes most of humanity from the good life. Today, 5 percent of humanity enjoys 95 percent of the wealth. That this is acceptable to anyone is a form of insanity and does not make any sense whatsoever. Yet, this is the way it is for us as the family of humanity. People are so egocentric that they fail to get and understand what the Christ actually is. The Christ is and means collective consciousness. For humanity, this means people living a collective state of existence whereby everyone is treated equal and equally shares in what is considered abundance. This requires all needs being met before this will happen. This is the true role of government, to provide its citizens with the basic necessities

Invading the Indigenous while the Rest of Us Watch

for living, food, clothing, shelter, transportation, education, and free health care.

The role of government is to implement ideas that meet the needs of the citizens it governs. Social failure is the legacy of most governments. Most subscribe to the invader culture way of life. Great emphasis is placed on a standing military. Economics based on monetary exchange and acquisition predominates. Class distinction is the aspiration for those overly tied to money and all it stands for. Those living at or below the poverty level comprise most of society. Getting ahead in life according to the dictate of survival of the fittest fuels social evolution. "God rewards those who succeed" is the motto subscribed to. Also the idea is to take advantage of others under the premise it is in their best interest that it is done.

Technology dazzles us. It convinces us we are intelligent and evolved. Nature and its creatures are what we measure our ability to think and create by. We believe we can conquer and control nature and the natural way of existence. We are determined to completely replace the natural environment with cities composed of steel, glass, plastic, cement, and asphalt. These are versions of Sodom and Gomorrah. Slowly, all traces of biological life are being converted into great cities hosting millions of people. Never mind the advice given to us was not to create places where people live that consist of more than two thousand inhabitants. We measure how evolved we are by how technological we are, how strong our military is, how much money is in circulation, and how many people are making good money. Never mind that our biology as our life is laid to rest.

These are irrelevant to our evolution personally and socially. Love and wisdom are not measured by anything other than how well we live and share these qualities. Lacking these, people are foolish and only accomplish death after great struggle. Notice that we do not take anything with us when we go. Only what truly exists evolves. In this measure, most of humanity has failed to get it, so personal evolution does not happen very quickly, if at all. But, then, that is how the invader culture wants it to be for us---our continuing to live that which self-destructs by our subscribing to ideologies having conquered and enslaved us through denial, pain, fear, guilt, and ignorance. These catalysts are the essentials for how the invader culture thrives--no one questions the absurdities of the insanity that compose the entire invader culture folly, with its emphasis on war, greed, and class distinction. This leads to disconnection and disintegration.

Every nation that has lived this way rises to 'greatness, only to crash and burn eventually. Self-destruction is the natural evolution of every invader culture nation. On a personal level, this is the death experience, which is not natural to our state of being. Life, its death a fiction, will only go to that place/state that mirrors the insanity one adopted as hiser life. Some call this heaven. What is lived down here is taken with us when we get up there. Lacking a working knowledge of the self/ ego, one is only capable of believing in ideologies that are the figments of the imagination of educated souls that are clueless as to what is real and true humanly. Lemmings are easily led astray by carrots never reached, held by individuals that 'Madoll" our attention, money, and livelihood.

A word to the wise for people who are successful in business: If what you are doing is not assisting people in their evolution, then you are simply taking advantage of them to your own selfish and arrogant end. It is as if we have set up a tollbooth between our inner self and outer ego on the journey of life lived on this planet. The type of booth we have set up differs from person to person, depending upon what is given meaning and value by us. Differentiation is paramount to us at the cost of commonness. I call this the syndrome of the king and queen. It is glorifying and idolizing the ego--at the cost of life itself. Almost all of humanity falls victim to this nonsense.

Birth, crucifixion, death, and reincarnation are the ways of individuals, society, and the nation state, when the invader culture mindset is lived as an ongoing ideal. Death of the body is reincarnation of the soul. They are identical experiences. Everyone that has left hiser body behind will have to reincarnate again, and again, and again. Ascension is, and means, "to rise above, take with, and integrate into." What we rise above are lower forms of consciousness.

Invading the Indigenous while the Rest of Us Watch

What we take with us is our body. What we integrate into is the larger community of the universe with a conscious mind. The body is only a representation of love lived according to this ideal. Just as the spirit is light individuated. These are our embodied spirituality. Love/light are our humanness. They are inversely reversed into male and female. As each one of us is unified, we become the oneness/perfection of Love/Light- light/love, humanly portrayed. Love/light, light/love is a concept from the RA Material/Law of One.

****

Information is pointless if it lacks the ability to evolve us. Much of what we think of as truth and reality are fictions of self-serving malcontents doing the bidding of That that has conquered and enslaved us to mindlessness and indifference, taking us to the grave after much struggle and suffering. By our own choosing, mind you! The common affliction of attitude for almost everyone is that we do not understand, or we don't want to hear it, or both. Wise teachers come, bringing new truths, and we staunchly refuse to listen to them and then make up ideologies about them, like we have done with every major religion, and especially the life of Jesus.

Alice Bailey was astute in the premise that Hinduism gave rise to Buddhism, and Buddhism gave rise to Christianity. I have added Christianity gave rise to the New Age Movement. Why? Hinduism focuses exclusively upon God and ignores life and humanness. Buddhism focuses upon life and completely ignores God and humanness. Christianity focuses upon a false god, ignores/denies life, misunderstands who the Christ is personally and socially, and is clueless about the soul, holding dogmatically to the propagandas that are figments of the imagination of misguided souls, duped by the self-serving under the premise of covenanted collusion. This is the basis for the traditions we honor and respect and for which we die.

There is only the family of humanity existing as the collective consciousness, called the Christ. On a personal level, the Christ is the third chakra. To fully activate it, one must know him or herself as all of humanity. The third chakra is also that which corresponds to our basic pattern or design. Most people are stuck in their first chakra, so most of what we are is denied, rejected, feared, or considered Satanic or "of and pertaining to the Devil." Few question what they are taught through traditions designed to keep us ignorant and very afraid. These traditions are currently very successful, and oblivious to their extinction.

The book of Revelation is a warning to all of humanity that our refusal to love, forgive, and do unto others results in what it shares as Jesus' vision recorded by St. John. Jesus' life, teaching, and vision were intended to end military, money, and hatred by 2012. Humanity was given two thousand years to accomplish this. Now, humanity is faced with the karma for refusing to return to living as designed by what Yahweh created and Id brought to life. Yahweh is the name of our creator, and Id is the name of what brought us to life 75,000 years ago. Id is our bestower, that which brought us to life. According to the RA Material/Law of One, humanness, as we are, was created and brought to life 75,000 years ago. The Mayan Calendars are records of this, as well as of our entire evolution up to 2012. This is the year the warlord god Jehovah and Id return to battle one last time. Those who support and subscribe to the ideologies of Jehovah will be taken at this time. According to Ramtha, this battle will last seven days, not seven years.

The entire point of the invader culture is to see how successful it is in deceiving us through the traditional forms of propaganda it has used for thousands of years. The predictions of and prophesies about the end times are warnings to us all to cease and desist in continuing to support that which only ends through self- destruction. We have staunchly refused to resolve the invader culture mindset as a point of view and engagement, so we face our doom, our extinction. Those who become extinct make up 99.3 percent of the human species. This is the number that has come to me intuitively. There is also the Bible versus that states: "The first shall be last, and the last shall be first." The first people are the indigenous that became what

Invading the Indigenous while the Rest of Us Watch

are now the last people. The last people now will become the first people again. This is the law of reciprocal-ness that will return the indigenous to their rightful place very soon. Humanity will return to living as it was created to exist as humanly, which is according to the will of God; love of Yahweh; light of Id; and the consciousness of all that is as the soul.

War, greed, and class distinction remain unchanged. Our human design remains unknown and unrecognized. Death is more appealing than life itself. The human drama continues its mindless confusion and incessant mass hysteria of disease, poverty, violence, destruction, animosity, and death. God created life; we create our own death experience.

Humanity is the Christ family when the people comprising it live the love/ light they are as a shared experience. This requires the willingness to get along and contribute to others without selfish motives. As it now stands, we live at odds with all that is. It is individuality in conflict with itself and all else. It is like we are in competition with each other through the notions of survival of the fittest, good versus evil, chosen-ness, and the belief that we are superior to others by the grace of God and genetics.

There is only one of us here, and each of us is that one. We only recognize in others what we are guilty of ourselves. How we interact with others is how we feel and think about ourselves. Our failure to see ourselves as others is the success of the invader culture propaganda. Hatred is the great legacy of the invader culture mentality, coupled with arrogance and selfishness. These were established through the religious and scientific ideologies of yesteryear. Unresolved denial and fear maintain every ideology that graves us to heaven, all for the sake of keeping up with the Joneses and setting ourselves apart from others.

What endears us to our own humanity? It is acceptance of our biology and fundamental nature. It is also resolving everything that makes us feel less than beautiful and wonderful just being alive. To do so requires process resolution of emotional causation. This is examining everything we feel and think, and resolving that which is contrary to our designed intention, which is the evolution of love/light, as a human representation, into what is unified, connected, and ongoing,

The invader culture lives antithetically to this. Modern day civilization represents the invader culture mindset through every nation state in existence. Contrary to this are indigenous people. They are our original design according to Yahweh and Id. Native peoples are how we were created to live humanly. The goal of the invader culture mindset is replacing everything natural with things artificial, like plastic, steel, glass, chemicals, medicine, and technology. This is the meaning within the idea of Sodom and Gomorrah. Ultimately, what replaces the human are robots and cloning. Biology is replaced with all things manmade under the guise of progress and "what is meant to be." We are convinced our way is superior to how we were created to exist, humanly. People now live like they are robots, puppets, and zombies. Soon cloning and robots will replace humanity with manmade ideals that have no soul.

Humanly, we are left to whatever choices we feel make our life worthwhile. Most of us are overly tied to our ego, family, karma, and psychologies of discontent. We surround ourselves with people, places, and things to reinforce our points of view. Intuition is discounted and discredited in exchange for the intellection of others qualified within the ideologies of science, religion, government, business, education, law and medicine. We ignore infinity. Our egoist convictions are so strong that we only allow certain ideas to predominate our way of life. This becomes oxymoronic when millions and billions of people subscribe to either scientific or religious views. No two people are the same, so it is impossible for two or more people to live the same way ideologically. Yet billions follow century old ideologies through faith and dogmatic conviction.

Invading the Indigenous while the Rest of Us Watch

Maintaining the Invader Culture:

Negative, Positive, and Arbitrary; Death/Fear and Life; Intuition and Propaganda; Conflict and Balance; Individuality and Oneness

We have to ask ourselves why we choose to deny our own reality and truth for ideologies that only have meaning and value to those who are or were the original thinkers and the intentions within their agendas.

Individuality demonstrates infinity humanly. All forms of diversity showcase infinity. Infinity is and means variability and variety of that which remains constant. God is the constant. What is the constancy of change? Certainty! But of what can one be certain? Only what is experienced as and within the medium one finds oneself existing as. In our case, it is our humanity.

Humanness is God-manifested consciousness existing as an ideal created and brought to life on this planet according to this biology. It is a fourfold representation consisting of three kinds of people, according to two genders. People are the human representation of mind, body, spirit, and soul. People live according to the invader culture mindset, the indigenous, or "the rest of us." Added to this are male and female. Humanly, we are the oneness/perfection of God, planet, and universe. We give this tri-unity its humanness. Humanly, we are the unified field theory.

Douglas H. Melloy

These three ways of living can be thought of as the negative, the positive, or the arbitrary. In a Christian sense, this can be thought of as the Old Testament way of life, the life of Jesus, or the complete arbitrariness of Paul. The irony of humanness is the sheep factor that puppets people and makes them either robotic and/or zombies. To prevent this from happening as one's life, one is wise to actualize and demonstrate what is real and true humanly as one's path of purpose. This requires going within to discover what humanness is and what it does, always against the status quo mentality of institutionalized tradition.

The role and purpose of science is the denial of the existence of God. The role and purpose of religion is teaching false doctrine about God. Every religion accomplishes this perfectly. The role of education is teaching us ideas that have nothing to do with our humanness as it is designed to exist humanly. The role and purpose of business is maintaining the art of greed. The role and purpose of politics is ensuring selfishness remains unchanged. The role and purpose of law is keeping the belief of good versus evil intact and in place. The role and purpose of medicine is convincing us that sickness and disease are our true state and nature. It is according to the invader culture, not so according to living indigenously. Maintaining false doctrine is why traditional institutions exist. According to David Icke, both science and religion originated out of the same school of thought. Disease is the outcome of people living the invader culture mindset.

No one questions these fictions of the self-serving who are institutionalized through tradition.

It is up to each of us to figure out who we are. If I were to ask someone what the name of the creator is, and the name of that which brought us to life, I doubt anyone now could answer this question accurately. There are approximately ten thousand gods worshipped on this planet, and none of them correspond to our creator that created us, and the bestower, which brought us to life. Christians believe that the warlord god Jehovah and Jesus are the same as "the one true God," but this is untrue. Neither is. These false gods, as

Invading the Indigenous while the Rest of Us Watch

they are used religiously, are forms and versions of the ego, which are denied and projected into an absolute that are worshipped and deified. Anytime an idol is worshipped, it is a version of the ego idolized and glorified. They are all graven images and idols. The ego is the face of denial and the basis for all things external that it then seeks to get from through worship and blind obedience.

This is what the invader culture has accomplished through religion. Four of them hold the attention of five and half billion people. They are Hinduism, Buddhism, Christianity, and Islam. The irony of this is that none of the teachers of what became the religions now practiced can move on until the ideologies of ignorance and arrogance are eliminated through healing and evolving beyond them. Every source that contributes to this planet is responsible for what is shared and what it evolves into. This is true for people as well. For anything that becomes negative over time, it is the responsibility of that source that introduced the ideas to do whatever it takes to eliminate the negativity.

Jesus cannot move on until we all stop believing false ideas about him and his life and teaching. True also of Buddha and Mohammad and anyone else who is the source of an ideology that is more fiction than fact. This is the basis for the idea of karma.

Karma is the effect of actions on our life over and through time and space. It is also the basis for the idea of atonement. We are responsible for the effects of what we feel, think, and act upon humanly. Anything negative involving others through us is our future karma. As I previously stated, this is why reincarnation happens. Death of the body is reincarnation of the soul. They are the same experience. Death is only possible when we are conquered and enslaved to what destroys our body by our refusal to live as designed. Reincarnation is only possible when a soul thinks of itself as merely a body. As long as the body dies, the soul will have to reincarnate. This is true of anyone who has left hiser body behind, including Jesus, Buddha, etc.

Life is created and is eternal by design. When life is lived as the love and light it is, death is impossible. It is only fear as our ego that makes death a possibility. Death is the ego getting even with itself by taking the body with it. The ego gives the body its sense of identity. The irony of this is that our mind creates our body, which the spirit brings to life, and that the ego then assumes is its life. The soul incarnates into the body and assumes consciously that it is the nature of the self. The work done in consciousness is remembering who we are as the image and likeness of God.

Not easy to do. The invader culture, with its magnificent seven traditions, convince us that war, greed, and class distinction, coupled with disease, competition, and contrariness, are the ways of our fallen-ness. Looking around, people seek to fit in at all costs, so they attach themselves to outer-based sources of information-all for the sake of attention, acceptance, and recognition by family, friends, and peers. This is the ego at work. The irony of this is that so many people now die due to exclusion of God, negation of life, and aversion to human being-ness. The cure is inclusion of God, affirmation of life, and involvement with humanness as it is designed to exist on this planet. That is accomplished when the ego is resolved by letting it go. How the ego is let go of is when one realizes they are in possession of what is real, true, and ongoing, and when one commits him or her self to becoming conscious of the inner and then sharing that as path and purpose. This requires ending the egos constant need for getting from others something it feels it is lacking or in need of.

The invader culture is all about artificial arbitrariness believed dogmatically as fact through traditionalized institutions. Quantum physics is actually the search for God. Astronomy is the study of the soul. All we accomplish is denial projected into absolutes that mean and tell us nothing about whom we are and why we are here. Evolution of our species is why we are here. The only aspect of humanness that evolves is what ascends, either individually or collectively. Very few people now are capable of ascending individually. Humanity is about one thousand years away from collective ascension.

Invading the Indigenous while the Rest of Us Watch

Collective awareness requires resolving the ego. Personally, collective consciousness is God, planet, and universe lived as self/ego. Socially, collective consciousness is the Christ. The soul is the collective consciousness of all that is specified. This is the oneness and perfection of being that knows, shares, and ascends. Making a contribution only matters when it assists others in evolving beyond the invader culture mindset and the limitations of the ego. This requires our knowing the differences between the self and the ego. There are many.

The invader culture is based upon the beliefs of hierarchy, elitism, superiority, chosen-ness, and good versus evil, leading to the social behaviors of conquering, enslaving, and destroying others through the ideologies of science, religion, politics, law, and business. These are in place traditionally to ensure that the invader culture mindset never diminishes or comes to an end. The end times predicted by some are only the insights of wise souls who understand that the entire fiction and figment of the invader culture comes to an abrupt end soon. It is very possible that most of us will see this by 2012. Invaders beware, as your days are numbered. Of course, so are ours if we are going to die.

Dying leads to death; living leads to ascension. We each decide which we will accomplish. The race is on now as to which will happen first, annihilation of life on this planet through pollution or through nuclear weapons. Unabated, we continue to pollute and make weapons of mass destruction-all under the guise that we are civilized and evolved. This is insanity, folks. We miss the point entirely of what life is and how we are the humanness of this biology. We refuse to accept and own love and light as our embodied spirituality. We refuse to know that our mind is the will of God, and that our soul is the universe. Will, love, light, and consciousness are our human being-ness lived personally. These four states of being are infinite, eternal, complete, and total as-is. Living love humanly ends the need for anything that kills and destroys, like disease, bullets, and bombs.

Douglas H. Melloy

The invader culture convinces us otherwise by teaching us that the mind is another name for the ego. Our body dies due to our unwillingness to heal our fear. The cause of death of our body is fear. Darkness is our spirituality. Our soul remains unknown to us for an entire lifetime, even after we have died and gone to the figments of our imagination. Some call this dying and going to heaven. Every soul of every human being comes from somewhere within the universe. It is our responsibility to remember and know our own soul before we pass on. I recommend reading Robert Monroe's book, Journeys Out of the Body. Rather curious how much stuff people believe that is only false doctrine. This is especially true of information that is designed only as propaganda to see if we will believe it for our entire life. Most of us do just that.

Then, we do something humanly that is insane. We actually have the audacity of taking the lives of others who disagree with our so-called sacred tenets or who do not follow arbitrary laws to the letter. Much of what comprises a given invader culture is based upon ideals that foster hatred, animosity, disparity, guilt, ignorance, arrogance, competition, fear, pain, addiction, dysfunction, distraction, intolerance, denial, indifference, and seriousness. To the invader culture mindset, humanness is not allowed. This is why the historicity of the invader culture is warring against indigenous people, who are the blueprint of our human design. Indigenous people are how we were originally created to exist humanly. We outsiders have missed this point entirely. The 'second coming' is our returning to living as designed as the Christ.

This requires the extinction of the invader culture mindset and all it entails. Again, the three main culprits of this way of life are fear, judgment, and persecution, which are the ways of the Old Testament, as covenanted by the warlord god Jehovah and his chosen people. The irony is this led to the life of Jesus and what he taught love, forgiveness, and doing unto others. Jesus' ideas were intended to heal the ways of the Old Testament, with its emphasis on war, greed, and class distinction. Obviously, this did not happen, so humanity is faced with the return of Jehovah for His chosen, which

Invading the Indigenous while the Rest of Us Watch

are all the people involved with supporting what composes the invader culture, which are military, money, and the elitist hierarchy. Hierarchy, elitism, superiority, chosen-ness, and good versus evil are the underlying ideologies of the invader culture, leading to the social behaviors of conquering, enslaving, and destroying others. "Taking possession of" is the protocol of the invader culture, because the people living this way have been "taken possession of" by the ideologies composing the invader culture mindset through subscribing to what science, religion, politics, business, education, law, and medicine represent as outer based ideologies that ensure people die, rather than ascend. It is the ego that feels the need to get from, so it becomes what is "taken possession of" by ideologies that are self-centered and very selfish and self-serving.

In a medium that is infinite, nothing has greater or lesser value than anything else. A grain of sand has as much relevance, existence-wise, as anything else. Infinity invalidates hierarchy and elitism, as well as everything else pertaining to the invader culture mindset. Universe, infinity, and all that is each state the same thing. There is only the oneness of God and all that this encompasses. People are blinded to this through the successes of institutionalized traditions revered as beyond reproach and question.

Most people are clueless as to what actually is going on and why. Humanity is now faced with the karma for its refusal to end what very soon becomes extinct here. It is the responsibility of each of us for being what is real, knowing what is true humanly, and then sharing that with others in ways that are kind and conducive. Lacking this shows that one is actually un-evolved, for it is only that which contributes to God's infinitude that has any value or relevance. Infinity is the diversification of God's all encompassing-ness into that which we observe as the universe. What we do to anything else is what we do to God. That is why Jesus stated: "Unto the least of these, ye do unto Me." 'Me' pertains to God, not Jesus.

Again, false doctrine is the way of the invader culture. This way of life is maintained through traditional ideologies existing as institutions. Success is measured by how many people subscribe to traditional points of view, which only exist to keep people steeped in dogmas that are merely forms of propaganda. Intuition is denied and ignored. Outer-based sources are the only ones considered reliable by the ego. The external is deemed what is real and true by the ego. The ego, and its ability to reason through observation, are what carrot us over cliffs, like lemmings. The ego is the past, present, and future humanized. His story becomes history. The outer only mirrors back to us what is inherent. The ego is convinced the outer is the reality, not the reflection. Our ego is the reflection of our body according to the soul's blueprint that the spirit brings to life as our karma and experience according to our own mind. In the context of like attracts like, the ego and the reflection are perfect mirrors of/as each other, both are illusions.

****

Why is it that large numbers of people choose to subscribe to notions of irrelevance? The body is the effect of the mind, and the ego is the effect of the body, so all the systems theories governing us are pure fictions of conviction dogmatically revered as truth and the way it is according to the ego. The adjustments we make are very slight, so nothing actually changes for us. This requires the death experience, so that we can get on with our reality unbiased by the figments of unenlightened minds honored and respected by centuries- old institutions. The elixirs of the conniving are many. The ego is drawn to what it feels most closely resembles it.

If something does not have the ability to sustain itself indefinitely, why do we use it as the basis of our culture? If we rely solely upon negative externals, we are doomed. This is what the invader culture has accomplished through money and social status. Class distinction is the hallmark of the ego and its need for acceptance, attention, and recognition by others. This requires the denial of God, planet, and universe as our self/ego. Universals require specific-ness in order for them to have any relevance or workability. Conflict is the result of complexity at odds with simplicity as a human ideal.

Invading the Indigenous while the Rest of Us Watch

Coupled with this is holding to an either/or mindset. These two ways of being make human experience dramatic and diseased. Disease is living life contrary to its design as our biology. The indigenous live their biology, so it remains healthy and disease free. The art of the invader culture is seeing how successful it can be in making us discontent and ill- at-ease with our own sense of humanness.

The invader culture and the indigenous exist so that people have the opportunity to choose this way of life as their polarity. Polarity is what the neutral becomes through development and discipline. What people misunderstand about energy is that it is the equality and balance between the positive and the negative existing as a neutral state. This becomes manipulated into good versus evil within the psychology of the invader culture. Good versus evil is the belief about positive and negative energy through bias. Bias is necessary in order for choice and wisdom to occur. When energy is misconstrued as good versus evil this established conflict within, so that peace and harmony cease to exist as one's life humanly. The end result is disease, violence, and war.

From the perspective of the invader culture, negativity is eternal and the way it is. The positive is despised and considered weakness. Ruthlessness is the measure by which the seeker is considered acceptable. Those who aspire to self-service find success in how well they subjugate others and convince people that going to war is the answer for nationalism. The warrior mentality is the measure by which the invader culture thrives due to the so-called superiority of those who choose to go to war against infidels, heathens, or pagans. Under the guise of being at war with some imagined evil that perpetrates acts of violence by the very agencies claiming to be at war against such. Successful conflict is guaranteed because one agency is playing both sides against each other under the guise of 'diplomacy. The real instigators are the ones who claim to be against, when they are actually the culprits behind what is going on.

Enculturation is a curious process. The ideologies of a select few are superimposed upon many. This is the basis for modern

Douglas H. Melloy

society existing as the nation state, with its large-population cities. Success is measured by impoverishment, crime, violence, disease, disparity, and dysfunctionalism. The catch phrase of every invader culture is, "survival of the fittest." It is very possible that the idea of Sodom and Gomorrah pertains to the cities and towns, even the concept of nation that now populate this planet.

What differentiates people is what they contribute to others. Getting or giving is the way of negative or positive polarity. What one contributes is the measure by which he or she demonstrates hiser evolution. What we aspire to shows how evolved or un-evolved we are in and as our human being-ness. The ego insists it can only get from, rather than own what one is in possession of that is contributed to others.

Are we at peace or in conflict with our humanness? Are we at odds with the biology of this planet? How predominant are addiction, distraction, and dysfunction? Are we always needy, wanting, lacking, and wounded, with more always considered essential to the 'good life,' and always at the expense of others? Is success also measured by how codependent people become on ideology, technology, and the invader culture way of life? Are we slaves to the nuances of the game? The game is very straightforward. Something or someone conquers us, then enslaves us, and then destroys us. On a personal level, this is the death experience after we have suffered greatly through subscribing to an idea or a series of ideas. Energy conforms itself to whatever we feel, sense, think, and envision about ourselves according to all the ideologies within which we place our faith, desire, and intention. The ego is convinced only 'out there' exists. The inner nature of being is denied and feared to the death.

Reality is self-defined. Each one of us decides what's so about something. Billions place their faith in ideologies, like science and religion, yet no two people are the same, so the ideas of one are usually irrelevant to others. Uniqueness misunderstands conformity and the infinitude of individuality. God is all that is as I Am-ness that we humanize. People seek to fit in and be accepted, so they sacrifice themselves to the dogma of others. What is your truth,

Invading the Indigenous while the Rest of Us Watch

and when are you going to be it and share it with others? Many are too afraid to go it alone long enough to find out. The retention of fear is the measure by which the invader culture thrives. The art of self-service is controlled manipulation by those who desire empowerment through others. This requires negativity to be what people feel about themselves most of the time. The predominance of negativity humanly only shows us how successful the selfish are in their form of charades.

We are all cartoon characters in the mind of God. The dichotomy we all are faced with divides us between love and wisdom or fear and ignorance. Each of us chooses what our life will be, humanly. This determines what our experience will be, as and during this particular incarnation. The roles of war, greed, and class distinction, as the invader culture, are those aspects of existence that allow individuality to play the game of a false god needing to be worshipped. The ego gets to feel it is a god, idolized and worshipped by others who assume they are sinners falling short of the glory of God, or who feel they are helpless and victims of their own mind. Perpetrators only answer the calling of those who feel they are helpless. Perpetrators only respond to what each victim feels is hiser life. Often perpetrators mete out karma to those seen as victims. It is the ego that feels it is a 'victim' to its incessant sense of lack, need, want, and wound. Perpetrators come playing on what we feel as what is 'done' to us.

Law as a practice is only necessary for those who believe the fiction of good versus evil. Law is the game of the ego. It is only necessary due to a lack of love. Ethics, morality, and integrity are self-taught. Each of us decides what meaning and value are regarding the purpose and function of life as it pertains to our experiences. What gets in our way is busyness. For many, doing is only a form of distraction. It is the way the ego distracts itself from itself. The art of pondering is as important as anything on which we focus our attention. It is the principle means by which we reflect upon our experiences and glean insight that leads to wisdom and understanding about our human condition. The art of self-reflection is lost to many. There is me, the positive or the negative, what I feel, think, and act upon, then there is the social reinforcements that society feeds back to me as my involvement with the community with which I live.

There is only being God, knowing the universe, sharing our biology, and then ascending. This is the path through purpose when lived positively. The path is going within. Purpose is how the inherent is shared without too much emphasis placed on the ego. The ego is our negativity given an identity. The self is our positive side given identity. We get to choose which aspect of energy we humanly portray. What is the identity of our neutrality? Where does it exist? It is the space between the in breath and out breath. It exists as a place between love and fear.

Holographic structuring is made possible through the technique of inverse reversal. This is energy spiraling into a center that then reverses its direction until it reaches that point where it began. This closes the ideal into what rotates on an axis. When pulsation is added to this, holographic structuring begins within a medium that is infinite and eternal. The belief that these opposites, existing as a binary vibrancy, are in conflict is the basis for the invader culture and our death experience. Healing takes place when opposites are known as harmony, for they are the peace of what is. Peace is the equality and balance between what is and what is not humanly lived.

The invader culture thrives through any and all forms of conflict, coupled with the psychology of right and wrong, true and false, good and bad, etc. Infinity allows and makes possible anything/everything. Selfishness considers itself an absolute, an entity unto itself through the ego. This requires the nonexistence of God, life, humanness, and the universe as something personal and involved. Science is this philosophy. It is why science is a systems theory. Denying the existence of God through science and teaching false doctrines about God through all religions ensures the ego that it is a false god idolized and worshipped by others. This is why

Invading the Indigenous while the Rest of Us Watch

there are so many people alive today that we glorify and idolize in politics, business, music, art, movies, sports, etc.

The ego requires that people sacrifice and martyr their lives for the arrogance of the chosen few. This happens with almost everyone who is successful in hiser endeavors. The art of propaganda is how convincing we are in our carroting. This is called marketing. What is marketed is false doctrine claimed to be 'the' truth. It is only the figment of the imagination of an ego convinced it is a god. Then, we worship this false god until we die.

The success of the invader culture through religion is that over ten thousand gods are worshipped, and none of them are the creator and that which brought us to life. Not one of them! This ensures that the creator and bestower of humanity remain absent from our experience. Another affliction we all face is those self-serving entities that have enslaved us to their intention and point of view. There are many taking advantage of our ignorance and lack of self-esteem.

The cure for this is our insistence on being in communication with positive entities who are truly serving humanity's best interest. Ask only for those who come with love and light. Ask also if the entity comes to assist humanity in its collective ascension. I have found two types of entities are channeled individual or collective. I also have discovered that collective sources are positive and individual sources are more negative than positive. This is true of all forms of individuality. According to the RA Material/Law of One, individuality ceases to exist at the fourth octave of sixth density, for the fourth octave of sixth density requires a balance of love and light. Individuality is why infinity exists. The ego only focuses on absolutes, while the self is the collective nature of our existence.

Our conflict is the result of our living as both an ego and the self. This is the paradox of universality and specific-ness. The ego relies upon the ideas of others to think it is real and alive. The self requires the use of intuition for all of its knowledge and sense of knowing. Notice how the intuition is discounted as reliable by the egos of small-minded malcontents who are clueless. It is treated as something that cannot be trusted. The ego of misguidance convinces us we are being deceived in the same manner as we are by those only seeking to empower him or her self. The irony of this is that all the false gods we worship are outer versions of the ego, using denial, projection, and objectification to become something continually worshipped by fearful egos too blind and arrogant to see this foolishness. So, the various ego gods remain worshipped long after the individual has transformed into something completely different than what is worshipped.

Caution is suggested here for anyone aspiring to become another false god, saint, or worshipped soul. Remember that everyone who has contributed to this planet and its people in any manner or way are responsible for their ideas and what they become as a form of practice, and those who taught will not evolve beyond this planet until all the ideas are healed. This will happen only when people begin living their reality and truth by ceasing to rely on the ideas others have shared that now exist as traditionalized institutions, as well as on all the other systems theories that are propagated on this planet. This is accomplished by letting the ego go for what is within one's life.

****

Individuality is at odds with God, life, humanness, and the entire creation. This is the role the ego plays for each of us. As long as we hold onto it as strongly as we do, we will not survive. Dying and going to heaven are not how we are created to exist humanly. Science tells us there is nothing after we die. This is untrue. Religion tells us we go to that place that is completely different than life here. That is a lie. It is the responsibility of each of us to be and know what the mind, body, spirit, and soul exist as, humanly. Again, humanness is the union and oneness of God, planet, and universe. The mind is God, the body is this planet, the spirit is identity and our ability to move independently, and the soul is the universe. These four states

Invading the Indigenous while the Rest of Us Watch

are the oneness of God, planet, humanness, and the universe. They exist as our will, love, light, and consciousness. These make us the unified field theory.

Humanly, we are the will of God as our mind, the love of the creator as our body, the light of the bestower as our spirit, and the consciousness of all that is as our soul. The role of the invader culture is to make sure we never know this about who we are. Its success is measured by what we believe about the mind, body, spirit, and soul that has nothing to do with these things. This ensures we will die. Death, destruction, and dysfunction are the ways of the invader culture. Competition, conflict, and violence are the only concerns of interest for the invader culture. The adrenaline rush people get from these behaviors is the only thing that matters, for nothing else exists to them. War, greed, and class distinction every society comprising the invader culture on this planet. Having a standing military, money as a form of exchange, and a wealthy class, contrasted by those living in poverty, are the measures by which the invader culture stands. Wisdom, artistry, and kindness are the measures by which a truly evolving person or culture stands. These are the highest ideals people can aspire to humanly. When everyone living lives this way, collective ascension is possible. Living love's acceptance and light's even-mindedness are the two highest attitudes humanly possible to exist as individually.

Stark individuality is the most important role anyone can play humanly within an invader culture. This is the idea behind, "the one true God." This is the warlord god of the Old Testament. It is a type of superego. The aspiration of some is to become just like this entity. Anyone who lives overly egoistically has the potential for becoming another kind of Jehovah.

Contrasted to this is the oneness of God, which is the entire universe and our human being-ness. The irony of this is that anything we do to anything else is what we do to God. A useful meditation is breathing in the idea of oneness, and then exhaling the idea of perfection. Do this until the experiences of both transpire. What we are is being God, knowing the universe, sharing this with others, and then ascending into a larger medium where our type of service can be used. Only that which serves has any usefulness to the creation. It is only this that evolves positively.

Knowing the sell/ego, contributing to others, and ascending the body are true human evolution. These are contrasted by the invader culture, with its denial, selfishness, and dying. The arts of conquering people through propagandist ideology, enslaving them to ideals that fail, and maintaining wars between people are the legacies of invader cultures historically. These remain unchanged now due to people not questioning what is actually going on. Obediently, we follow the dictates of the ideals of traditions that exist to maintain the city/nation states that every invader culture needs to thrive as a version of Sodom and Gomorrah.

Invading the Indigenous while the Rest of Us Watch

Humanity and the Invader Culture:

God; Love and Light/Yahweh and Id; Free Will; Ego and Self; Reality; Original Design; Evolution; Nature

First, humanity was conquered by the warlord god Jehovah through a hierarchical/elitist ideology. Second, humanity became enslaved to this ideology as religious doctrine through the conviction that they were His chosen people, which remains in place to this day. Third will be the destruction of Jehovah's people when this entity fulfills Its promise and returns for everyone that is maintaining a faith that is only the propaganda of the invader culture as it exists and thrives on this planet today. The unsuspecting will be caught unaware. It is very possible that December, 2012 is the year of Jehovah's return.

Again, according to the Seth Material, as channeled by Jane Roberts, "Retention of the Star of David and recreation of the state of Israel necessitate the return of Jehovah for His people." Does this make the Jews the bad guys? Heaven's no! They had no way of knowing that their God was, in fact, a warlord that conquered them, enslaved them, and will destroy them for keeping the faith intact and in place until now. Christians also have accomplished the same thing through their Bible and religiosity, which is contrary to what Jesus taught. Jesus taught love, forgiveness, and doing unto others to resolve the Old Testament ways of fear, judgment, and persecution. These three ideologies are how the invader culture works with the masses.

Anyone interested in going to war only does the bidding of Jehovah. This is how one knows that the individual is self-serving. When the interest is in class distinction and greed, this also lets us know the person is very negative and selfish. The hierarchical nature of kings, queens, sirs, dukes, knights, etc. also showcase for us the roles played in invader cultures. History has shown us how the invader culture works from culture to culture through the superpowers of their day. The fact that people allow this as a social way of life is sad and very reprehensible.

The end of the world only pertains to and involves the invader culture and all who engage in what it is as a social aberration. It is the great social fiction and lie that most of humanity dies for. God does not create and then destroy. I do not see fit to kill what God decided to create as Its reality and truth. Everything and everyone is an aspect and quality of God. What I do to any aspect of the creation on this planet is what I do to God. Every species in existence has the same right to life as I do. I choose to love and appreciate God's various identities, which demonstrate what infinity is on this planet. Evolution does the same thing. It shows us how 'what is' changes from generation to generation.

Those who attribute death and destruction to God do not know what they are talking about ever! There is only the self-sustaining, self-regenerating, and self- perpetuating, according to the instantaneous, spontaneous, and simultaneousness of God now here being. This is the eternal ongoing-ness of God's infinitude that we observe as our humanity, this planet, and the universe. The irony of all this is that we have confused and deluded ourselves into thinking we are the most evolved and intelligent thing within the entire universe. We arrogantly state this through science and our ego's ability to conjecture. Some actually believe we are the only form of intelligence in existence. We staunchly hold to the fictions of past, present, and future. Where is the past now? Where is the present now? Where is the future now? They do not exist except as memory

Invading the Indigenous while the Rest of Us Watch

and imagination. Events are recorded for karma purposes only. What has come and gone no longer exists. Our memory of it is only our interpretation of it, and experiences differ from person to person. Especially when people are involved with the same experience.

Ask a number of people what happened and you'll get as many different versions as there are people asked. Humanness is as much individuality as it is collective and relational. This is by design. Humanness involves the personal, relational, social, global, and universal. All five states of being are involved simultaneously. It is only our attachment to the ego that limits our awareness and keeps us ignorant about other aspects of our life that are just as real and relevant. Because quantum physics is actually the search for God and astronomy is actually the study of the soul, from a place of denial and projection, this ensures that God as our mind and the universe as our soul are never known and lived as such, humanly.

It is very curious how people are punished to the death for things. We see this everywhere now. Religion is the greatest culprit of this for many cultures living on this planet. Love accepts everything as-is. Fear does the opposite. Everything and everyone is considered a threat to its existence. The ego is the fall guy for each of us. It takes the body with it as its hostage. Death is the ego getting even with itself. Death is a form of suicide. It is how we take our own life, for our refusing to live as the image and likeness of God. The eternal nature of the self requires death so that we can become one with our existence. If we are left to our current life without death, we would remain this way forever. Few evolve into who they are as God and universe unified into a single state of being that knows making one's humanness the unified field theory.

Many do not know where God is within. Many do not know their own soul. Many do not allow themselves to be love as their body and know light as their spirituality. I call this embodied spirituality. Love is the physical. Light is the spiritual. These are coupled with fear and darkness so that we can live as male and female. The feminine is to love what the masculine is to light. Love and light as divinity and deity correspond to our creator and bestower. Their names are Yahweh and Id. Yahweh created us, and Id brought us to life. Yahweh is a collective of thirteen beings. Id is a collective of twenty beings..

To those wondering why they are absent from our experience, free will is paramount to the creation. We all are allowed to believe whatever we wish to, humanly. Beginning with our biological parents, and then with our sense of identity as gender, race, family, karma, interest, and occupation, we are left alone in the hopes we will go it alone to discover who we are as the image and likeness of God through the love of Yahweh and light of Id. It is not easy to understand how divinity and deity are inversely reversed into our femininity and masculinity. It is like we are four beings in one. We are the union and oneness of these as our humanity. Oneness is not easy to experience or understand. There is the oneness of the ego and the oneness of the self. These exist as either an absolute through the ego or a collective as the self. It is the spirit that exists as oneness.

Few take the time to resolve their ego, so it remains the predominator of their lives, taken to the grave. The ego is the choice maker for each of us. It decides what's so about our life. It also gives specific-ness to what is all encompassing and infinite. God's true nature is all encompassing. This state became infinite as the universe. These two states became us as our humanity. We are the image and likeness of God and universe humanly on this planet.

The invader culture tells us otherwise, as always, through science, religion, education, business, politics, law, and medicine. It tells us all sorts of things that have little to do with our being-ness. The carroting of our awareness works very well. Few evolve beyond the ideologies of the invader culture. Few make the conscious decision to live simply and indigenously. We are consumed---from our fear, guilt, arrogance, and denial; to our sense of lack, need, want, and wound; to our addictions, dysfunctions, and distractions, seducing us into maintaining them to the death. Many do not know any better. Many do not know how or where to begin in resolving their ego and self into a useful companionship.

Invading the Indigenous while the Rest of Us Watch

I remember the first time I heard the idea of soul mate. I did not like it. The only idea about this that makes any sense to me is that, when my soul incarnated into my body, it became mated to it. This is the only soul mate relationship I will ever have, humanly. Another idea posited that is false is twin flame. Love and light are the only twin flames that exist, so that my love and light, as my body and spirit, comprise the only twin flame, which is my life as my e embodied spirituality. These are coupled with my mind and soul. Another way of looking at our life is through the relationships between the mind/body, body/spirit, and spirit/soul. Self discovery requires a lot of work and going it alone.

The invader culture is very subtle at undermining people who are teachers of truth from a state of being what is real. Always our attention is outer-based through denial and fear, so that what predominates our life is all things negative and reprehensible. Negativity sells. People are convinced they are going to the grave, and the way it is. The Old Testament God Jehovah is to the universe what Hitler was to Germany. Yet every Christian believes to the death that this warlord created us and brought us to life as Adam and Eve. According to Edgar Cayce, seven root races were created at the same time. Each race corresponded to the colors of the rainbow. That makes sense to me in this context. Light is our spirituality. Humanness has a direct correlation to every color of the spectrum, as well as to darkness and white light.

We do not do a very good job in understanding the role catalysts play with our personal and social evolution. We thrive on playing the role of the victim. We attribute good deeds to God and bad things to Satan, the Devil, or Lucifer. Few accept responsibility for what hiser mind creates as experience, using both positive and negative energy, so that we can understand how energy works creatively. Willed intention is the basis for everything in existence. God's will to be and know is why the universe came into being. Everything composing the universe is God stating I Am.

The warlord god Jehovah convinced His chosen people that He is "the one true God."This was stated historically as, "I am that

Douglas H. Melloy

I am."This dooms the believers to a destructive end. This is the end result through that which conquers and enslaves. Everyone who dies goes through the same process without realizing it. The only states that exist are will, love, light, and consciousness, existing as our mind, body, spirit, and soul. These make us the image and likeness of God humanly and biologically. Love is the physical and is our body. It is the temple of the living God. This is why we are told Biblically, "Let the dead bury the dead; God is only of the living" Rather than understanding this statement of truth, we are more interested in dying and going to heaven. Many 'true believers' who preach do not like what they find once they have passed, only to discover heaven is what they make it, and not the way it is as the real and true.

Energy will conform itself to anything we believe. This means our reality and truth is what we feel, think, and act upon. This is true for all of us. Infinity is the fact that all things are possible. Infinity is God's individuality. Creation can be thought of as all encompassing, infinite, and specific simply, God, universe, and identity. How these are represented humanly involves what composes energy. People live according to what is negative, neutral, and positive. These determine all of our experiences at this level of being. Knowingness is the extension and expansion of energy from being into experiences that express what energy is as our life. What we choose to place our attention on determines our livelihood when coupled with intention. Faith is the evidence of things unseen. Desire develops our faith. Intention culminates in to the fruition of what our faith and desire is placed upon. This is the basis for all of our experiences.

The evolution of intelligence divides between controlled manipulation and creative manifestation. This also can be thought of as individuality at odds and at war with the rest of creation. This requires replacing what is natural with what is artificial. We observe this in the replacing of nature with cities and the polluting of the environment with chemicals and waste. The race is on with the invader culture as to what actually destroys this planet, nuclear

Invading the Indigenous while the Rest of Us Watch

warheads or pollution. The real culprit behind these two insanities is indifference to life and to our humanness. God, life, humanness, and contribution are left out of the equations we have factored as the way it is. The idea of Sodom and Gomorrah existing as the ity/nation state is this. It is the replacing of what is natural and created with ideologies that are nothing more than false doctrine.

The invader culture has succeeded in converting people into robots, zombies, and puppets. Few people today are truly authentic in their life. The obvious is missed. Few question the propagandas revered as science, religion, and education. So, this propaganda remains unchanged and unquestioned to the very end. Now, the indigenous and invader live side by side. Each presents its psychology as a way of life. The rest of us observe both without committing ourselves to either. We do not understand why there are indigenous people. We do not realize what the true intention is of the invader culture. We outsiders go about our business, oblivious to the invader culture and the ways of the indigenous. This is not without grave consequences for most of humanity.

Invader cultures are all about the enslavement and destruction of people, places, and things. This is their sole purpose. How this is accomplished is through false doctrine Da Vinci coded into dogmas of belief. This is done through ideologies written as systems theories of conviction. Most of the ideas are disseminated to keep us believing in theories whose intent is that we never live what is real and true as our human being-ness. Nothing remains the same, moment to moment, so why do we hold onto ideas that are older than the moment? Most religious and scientific beliefs are hundreds, if not thousands, of years old. The instantaneous is missed. The past has passed away, yet we hold onto it for dear life. The question is why, given that its passing demonstrated that it never truly existed, ever!

The disclaimer for everything stated and stipulated is: "Even this is propaganda, to see what you'll believe." Everything stated by another through radio, print, television, and movies states this for us. It is only the ego that decides what another says is true and the way it is. We then decide whether we want to believe that what another holds as reality and truth is that for us. This is impossible given the nature and role of infinity. No two people are the same, so why do billions believe in a given doctrine of faith, business practice, or political view? Few realize that every systems theory of the invader culture has conflict within it. Division is what conquers people. Again, the idea people hold onto is good versus evil. This allows the invader culture to thrive. Conflict exists to give people the opportunity to choose either the positive or the negative as one's way of being, knowing, and sharing. Refusing to polarize means one's life is arbitrary.

Notice how indigenous people remain true to their way of life to this day. Those who remain faithful are the wise ones, for they know that, one day, humanity will return to living indigenously. This is stated in the Bible as: "The first shall be last, and the last shall be first."They are our original design. The indigenous people are our true way of existing humanly. They are how we were created to live humanly. They were the first people who became the last, that one day will return to being the first people once again.

Science, religion, business, and politics have duped us into believing we are evolved and civilized, with our technology, cities, and nation states. Those are only representations of the ego made manifest. Nothing has actually changed humanly in eleven thousand years. Human evolution is measured by how it heals 'sin,' sickness, disease, and death. Also, by how it resolves the invader culture mindset into what is peaceful, harmonious, and ascendant. It is our responsibility to heal what is contrary to our true nature. Humanity was given two thousand years to end war, greed, and class distinction as social mores through the life of Jesus and his teaching. His vision, recorded as the Revelation, was a warning to all of humanity that refusal to end the invader culture mindset results in the extinction of everyone engaged and supporting ideologies of fear, guilt, arrogance, and denial disguised through science, religion, business, politics, education, law, and medicine.

What will people do when their world ends forever?

Invading the Indigenous while the Rest of Us Watch

Pray to Jesus, I suppose. How will the invader culture extinction happen? It will happen when oil and electricity are withdrawn. When does it take place? When Jehovah returns to finish what was 'promised' back then. One idea I was told by The Council of Layett was that oil was going to be withdrawn. When I asked what did they mean by oil, their response was: "Man's ability to understand will be removed." It is very possible this planet will change the parameters of how life will live on its surface. The changes that take place will have the same effect on people living the invader culture way of life as did that which caused the extinction of the dinosaurs. Life that is not compatible with what comes will fade away. This is also true of people outgrown by life through evolution into greater levels of love and light lived and expressed. Evolution is the development of consciousness through experience. This is the refining of awareness into what works. For us, it is our human being-ness. Each of us is evolving personally, relationally, and socially- unless we miss the point and purpose of why we exist as we do.

Only three kinds of people exist. They are invaders, indigenous, or the rest of us. Each type lives according to ideals that establish that way of life. As stated earlier, this can be thought of as living negatively, positively, or arbitrarily. The irony of this is that the Bible is in exactly the same format. The Old Testament is negative, the life of Jesus was positive, and the life of Paul was arbitrary. We choose which way we are going to live. This is the art of being and knowing,

Not easy, as everyone has hiser point of view. Everyone is entitled to live exactly as he or she chooses to live. This is the perfection inherent within the creation. It is why we are left to our own imagination. Free will is paramount to our existence. It is what allows each of us to experience and express whatever. The oxymoron is conformity. It negates our individuality into living like sheep- only following the status quo of misguided, selfish people. Missing the point, life passes us by and lays us to rest for our refusing to live life as it exists according to our true ideal.

Douglas H. Melloy

Death levels, or evens, the playing field for everyone. The ego is never recognized in the afterlife. This means it never truly existed in the first place. The ego is the mask energy wears as the body. The body is a representation of the mind according to this human ideal. It is created and brought to life so that Yahweh and Id are seen humanly as each one of us. Jehovah replaced our true parents as "the one true God."Two billion people today have the legacy of keeping the warlord god Jehovah tied to this planet. Almost all of humanity supports and subscribes to the legacies of war, greed, and class distinction through allowing the invader culture mindset of Jehovah to thrive now.

It is very possible that 99.3 percent of humanity will not survive what returns. The second coming is the return of humanity living its realness as a personal truth. This requires a returning to our true nature as designed by the love of Yahweh and the light of Id. These were inversely reversed as and through our biological parents. It is love/light inversely reversed as light/love.

****

Again, an irony of our humanness is how we rely solely upon outer-based sources for everything we believe in, through books, teachings, and teachers. It is the ego that does this. The inner, and all it entails, is denied and ignored. This is why God is not known and lived humanly. It is also why the universe is not known as our own soul. The ego has succeeded in objectifying itself into an absolute. The very rude then insist that their ego is the godliest, requiring that others bow down and worship what it considers itself to be. Many have played this charade in the past. Many play this charade right now. Such is the folly of misguided malcontents doomed to their own fear and ignorance. The ego is the charade we play to the death.

The ego only serves the purpose of giving God and universe a sense of specific- ness as it corresponds to our design and this planet. There is a direct relationship between our humanness and

Invading the Indigenous while the Rest of Us Watch

the biology of this planet. This is very difficult to understand. The invader culture has replaced what is "nature and us" with all sorts of artifacts that keep us distracted, dysfunctional, and addicted to them due to unresolved fear and our feeling that we do not belong here. We are addicted to our ego, so we do not get it about what is real and true humanly.

Humanness is an abomination to Jehovah. It is not allowed its true expression. This warlord hates our human being-ness. This is what the invader culture embodies through war, greed, and class distinction. Jehovah hates God also. This entity's sole purpose is discovering planets and converting intelligent life forms into mean, selfish, and aggressive tyrants that thrive on war and idolization. Many are recorded throughout our history. Anyone who has engaged in war is a human version of Jehovah. His dictates of covenant and conversion remain unchanged. Now, humanity is faced with its end times for refusing to end Jehovah as "the one true God."

This is the actual legacy of Judaism, Christianity, and Islam. Hinduism, Buddhism, and the New Age Movement also have their shortcomings. Few people accept the responsibility of embracing and owning their reality and truth and sharing that with others humbly and transparently. Even when wise souls come, like Jesus and Buddha, few aspire to be as loving and enlightened as they were, according to the love and light people are. We are addicted to our fear, guilt, and pain. Institutions stand just to reinforce what takes us to the grave. Trying to be and live like another is as ridiculous as it gets. What is your reality and truth, and when are you going to be it and know it, and then share such with others? Few will be able to answer this. Even less will choose to live the love and light that makes us the image and likeness of God. That is how successful Jehovah is through science, religion, education, business, politics, law, and medicine.

The year 2012 looms on the horizon, like the angel of death waiting to act. We all pretend we are ignorant of this outcome. Fingers will point, emotions will rise, and billions face this holocaust. Remember, though, that those who attribute) death and destruction to God do not know what they are talking about-ever! It is our own responsibility to look at what happens to us and to learn what we can from it. The holocaust of the Jews during WWII was the final opportunity for them as a people to examine what they worship as a religious ideology, as it is this and this alone that causes what comes for everyone who places their faith in ideas that pertain to and involve war, greed, and class distinction. Again, look no farther than the retention of the Star of David and the recreation of the state of Israel, which is specifically what brings about the return of the warlord god Jehovah to this planet by the end time of the Mayan Calendar. The dust will eventually settle, and those remaining will evolve into what collectively ascends.

People make the same mistake about Jesus, now, that was made during his lifetime. It is the idea that he comes to destroy the wicked, also the idea that he comes to judge people. Jesus was the messiah for the Jews. Love, forgiveness, and doing unto others are what resolve the attitudes of fear, judgment, and persecution that were needed for conquering, enslaving, and destroying others that was the early history of the Jews after their conversion to Jehovah's covenant. This also was the basis for the 'holy war. Others have adopted this notion as religious theology. The role of Jesus was the hope that humanity would end military, money, and self-glorification as personal and social orders of conduct. In this, his life was a failure. He did his best; we failed to get it.

Much of what we believe as sacred is sheer nonsense. Much of what we believe as scientific fact is pure folly and fiction. The ego thrives on insanity, so there is mindless war that accomplishes nothing. There is unmitigated greed that impoverishes 95 percent of humanity. There are the idolized egos of many kings and queens all puffed up and headed for the grave, taking as many with them as possible.

The key to success with the invader culture is how ignorant people are about the nature of the self, service polarity, and collective ascension. This is coupled with the arrogance of the ego. How easily and readily people believe in fictions, generation after generation

Invading the Indigenous while the Rest of Us Watch

and century after century, demonstrates the effectiveness of the propaganda used by those who only care about self-empowerment at the of others. This expense way of life can be very alluring to the unsuspecting. It is like the ego is asking, "Is my ego big enough to win?" Others set standards that many aspire to in the hopes of becoming as rich, or as famous, or as powerful. These are types of bait-carrots used to lemming people into following and never questioning what the actual agenda is that is worshipped and obeyed blindly. Success is also measured through the arts of reward and punishment and fear and guilt, played upon through manipulation. This ensures people are controlled into maintaining the agendas of the invader culture until the very end. This means military, money, and arrogance predominating until they become extinct at the end of 2012.

Money only exists as a form of exchange for class distinction. It is unnecessary. Bartering is the natural way of exchange. Equal value is given for equal value. This is life giving to life, humanly. The predation of animals is exactly the same thing. Predator and prey is life giving of itself completely to assist the evolution of both. Our egocentricity prevents us from understanding much of anything. We are blinded by self-serving agendas that are considered the way it is for us, humanly. Over and over, we see how the charades of the few affect and afflict the many. Few question what is actually going on, so the invader culture remains unchanged. So-called advances are made, but nothing actually changes within the invader culture. It remains standing until the empire falls by imploding upon itself. This is what history tells us year after year.

Great invader cultures rise, only to fall eventually. War and greed ensure nations will fail. America is next. It epitomizes the invader culture. It also holds the promise of the indigenous, who wait patiently for the invader way of life to end forever. This is the way of every planet that has created intelligence living and evolving. Both ideals evolve side by side. Everyone is given the chance of aspiring to become either an invader or an indigenous person. For those living arbitrarily, it is time for you to go home. It is time for you to pack up your soul and catch the next available UFO going to your part of the universe. Ah, but science tells us they do not exist, and that we are the only intelligence in the universe! This is taught to us in spite of the fact that thousands of details prove otherwise, like crops circles, the Great Pyramid, ancient drawings of astronauts, UFO sightings, Easter Island, etc.

Invading the Indigenous while the Rest of Us Watch

Invader Culture and the True Nature and Purpose of Humanity:

Fictional Beliefs; Forgiveness vs. Acceptance; Infinity; Human Beingness; Four States of Being; Experience; Religion

Belief is a very curious type of acceptance by the ego. Sometimes, what we believe is supported by some kind of fact or facts. Some beliefs we just want to be true, so we hold on to them, hoping that they prove to be correct. Some ideas we accept because we are expected to believe in them, like the Immaculate Conception, Jesus dying on the cross for our sins, that we landed on the moon, that Kennedy was assassinated by Oswald, that 9/11 was an act of terrorism by foreign nationals. The list goes on about ideas we believe that are not true. I'll go so far as to state that anything that the ego believes cannot be true because the ego does not exist. Yet, so much of what we believe is just the ego deciding to believe in something. Like the idea that Jehovah is a jealous God, our creator, and "the one true God." Love is never jealous about anything. This means Jehovah is not a true God, or our God. Jehovah is negativity existing as an absolute, so that those who feel that way about themselves can follow suit in aspiring to be as negative.

This is why the invader culture glorifies the ego as a god. Something that is nothing is given value and meaning. This is the art of arbitrariness treated as something serious and relevant. Can anyone who dies be taken seriously? No! Their fiction was greater than their reality and truth. I have met many selfish people who lack any real content of character. Many have considered themselves teachers and wise souls. Their arguments are strong and well thought out. Then, the work begins in invalidating one's entire life. The invader culture works the same way. It invalidates the ideas and life of anyone who chooses to live honorably according to our true identity. This is why persecution is so important to the invader culture psychology. It is also why law governs the land. Law is the technical side of persecution. Real criminals never go to jail. They are above the law, like David of the Old Testament. He broke all Ten Commandments and was still exonerated by God for doing so. Love, when lived, make laws unnecessary, always!

The letter of the law does not apply to those who pass them. This is as true for Jehovah as it is for those who govern. Many in positions of power are beyond the reach of the law. Law is primarily imposed to keep people enslaved. The threat of death is the guarantee of maintaining control over systems of injustice, like apartheid. Justice is a curious word, for it implies revenge by a source more powerful than we are. Justice, as an idea, is only possible when people live victimization. This is also true for the idea of forgiveness. Love only accepts. This renders forgiveness unnecessary. Karma is more useful as a teaching aid. These ideas are a moot point when creativity and intention are understood, also the agendas of others. In order for an agenda to work selfishly, people have to be against it. This is the conflict needed in order for what is resisted to stand. This is why we are taught, "What you resist, persists."

Another area of success for every invader culture is gender disparity. This is the idea that one gender is superior to another. Early in our history, it was women as the matriarchal; then, the balancing of that came into existence as the patriarchal. Invader cultures fail to realize that there is only equality and balance as the creation. In a medium that is infinite, nothing has greater value than anything else. A grain of sand has as much relevance and realness as a planet, sun, or galaxy. Value and meaning are arbitrary. Each of us gives the only

Invading the Indigenous while the Rest of Us Watch

meaning that something has. This is also true of value. Why money is the great determiner is very curious, given it has no inherent value. It is oxymoronic that money predominates our mindset as it does. Great wealth here is balanced by extreme poverty there. Our lack of understanding the facts of karma, equality, and balance only shows how un-evolved we actually are, humanly.

Evolution is how readily and quickly one changes hiser point of view and condition. Humanly, evolution is measured by how healed people are collectively. This requires the ending of the idea or notion of nation/city state, as well as the belief of opposites in conflict, like good versus evil. The real culprit behind this specific belief is hatred, and there is no such thing as good hatred and evil hatred. Each one of us is responsible for examining every belief held onto during our current incarnation. Most of what is believed, in the form of institutionalized traditions, is a version of the fiction that the world is flat. It is very curious how we make famous those people whose ideas add to accepted traditions. Then, we lemming ourselves to the death by believing and placing our faith in ideas designed and intended to do just that.

The path of almost everyone, humanly, is the idea of birth, crucifixion, death, and reincarnation. Death of the body is identical to reincarnation of the soul. If one leaves hiser body behind, he or she will reincarnate again. This process will continue for as long as it takes for one to resolve hiser human ideal into that which is eternal and ongoing.

****

When pondering human being-ness, which is only God-manifested consciousness, is very wise and useful to do so from the perspective of living as the image and likeness of God, rather than from the fiction that one is "a sinner falling short of the glory of God." Or from the scientific nonsense that we have evolved from nothing into something by chance occurrences, which is impossible. Something from nothing is a great fiction believed by so many.

Douglas H. Melloy

Another ridiculous notion is the argument that proof is possible through observation and intellectualization. Change makes proof impossible. It is only our blinded belief that makes a given idea stand alone as an accepted fact. Facts are fictions realized years too late.

The point of an idea is where it leads one. No idea is an end unto itself. Every idea leads to another, infinitely. Ideas are based upon what is first felt, and then thought to be what is so, for each of us. It is the way experiences unfold for us. Eventually, what is felt leads to God consciousness, and what is thought leads to universal awareness. This is being God and knowing the universe as the self humanly portrayed on this planet. This is what ascends only after service is given to others. Service is how people are assisted in ascending God/universe as one's being/ knowing. Lacking direct experience of both, these ideas are only points of truth unrealized and unlived by people who subscribe to what science tells us or what religion stipulates. Few question the validity of either figment, so they remain intact until the end of our invading days.

It is only the invader culture that ends here within our lifetime. This is the end of the world prophesied by so many throughout history. People do not realize how energy works, humanly. Again, the positive and negative aspects of energy are balanced into a biased neutrality that then must choose which force to polarize into, humanly. One then serves either the positive or the negative as hiser life purpose. This is referred to as holding the right or left hand of God. People are easily fooled by the deceptive nature of the invader culture. All kinds of enticements are used by the self-serving to ensure the naïve remain ignorant of the fact of what is actually going on through agenda and intention. This ensures nothing changes traditionally, such as competition, conflict, and ego glorification. These make individuality into all the false gods worshipped by duped aspirants all aspiring to become the next worshipped idol.

****

Invading the Indigenous while the Rest of Us Watch

Humanness involves four states of being. They are God, planet, universe, and self/ego. These are unified into a single state we each live as our life. This makes our life the oneness and perfection of God, planet, and universe existing as our self/ego. The path is how we discover what each is as our life, and how we live them consciously. Not easy to do, as the magnificent seven traditions governing our lives are designed to take us to the grave, after we fund them with our energy through our emotions and thoughts. A useful book to read about this is the Seth book, The Individual and the Nature of Mass Events. It eloquently explains how mass consciousness works between people and the environment.

Addiction, dysfunction, and distraction are three catalysts few outgrow or heal. Great cities rise only to fall, as do entire nations. Collapse is inevitable. Every great nation existing as an invader culture that rises to preeminence falls by imploding from living the fictions of militarization, money as economics, and class distinction. These are the great follies people die for through war, greed, and the belief they are God's chosen people. The specific-ness of the end of the world involves the belief a person or group is chosen by God as His favored sons and daughters. This idea is epitomized by the story of David in the Old Testament. Even after breaking all ten commandments, he is still exonerated by God. This is arrogance at its finest. Arrogance is another human trait few outgrow. Humility and transparency are essential if one hopes to truly evolve.

Paradox is natural to the universe. The reason why is: opposites exist as binary vibrancy so that God will experience specific-ness. This is the I Am-ness of God experiencing individuality. In dividing, you have God living infinitely. The technique used by God is inverse reversal. This is where a single state becomes a duality. We experience this in four ways, as the heartbeat; breathing; waking and sleeping; and incarnation and ascension. These four binary states exist simultaneously. We also observe binary vibrancy as male and female, light and dark, love and fear, etc. Nothing in the universe is an absolute-not even God! The ego and the selfish would have us believe otherwise. Every idol worshipped is a form and version of the ego. People have succeeded in remaking God into a super ego. This is the real art of the invader culture. Remake the entire creation into one grand figment that people die for. Most of humanity has done just that.

The end of the world and the death experience are identical. Only figments and fiction fade away into the nothingness they weren't. Reality and truth exist infinitely and eternally. When one lives what is real and true, ascension takes place. Until then, people come and go. This is called death and reincarnation. They exist only because people do not realize what their mind, body, spirit, and soul are, humanly. The mind is God; the body is this planet; the spirit is the moon; and the soul is the universe. These make us human beings. (The moon means four things as a symbol in this book. It represents oneness; our spiritual individuality identified; also, it is service polarity; and it is that which illuminates or keeps hidden from view.)

The seven traditional institutions of man tell us otherwise. They convince us to death that our life is other than and contrary to what is. People blindly accept what each of these traditions tells them. Few question the beliefs that culture is based upon. Especially when science and religion are involved. Many cultures use punishment to the death for daring to question self-serving ideas guised as religion. In this way, the warlord god Jehovah has been very successful. This god is jealous, which only means it is unloving and a hater of humans who image God as their true identity. It is impossible for God to be jealous, for God is love, and only accepts everything as what it is, that is simply God existing as ideals of I Am-ness. Jesus taught love, forgiveness, and doing unto others to end fear, judgment, and persecution. These are the Judaic and Old Testament ways of doing Jehovah's bidding. Love ends fear and all acts of war. Forgiveness ends all forms of judgment. Doing unto others end all forms of persecution.

Jesus did not understand that forgiveness is unnecessary when acceptance is truly lived. It is what love does, just as light remains even-minded about everything. Unresolved fear keeps the invader culture alive and well until it ceases to exist. This is why

Invading the Indigenous while the Rest of Us Watch

the end times are predicted by various sources. When the source making a prediction is tied to that which ends, this is recorded as the end of the world. What is meant is the end of the world believed in when what is believed is false, and not existing as it was created to represent. The end times come because reality and truth evolve beyond all the fictions people insist upon dying for. Illusions always fade away forever. As people, it is only those who die, never having lived in the first place.

This is the fate that waits for the invader culture and all who subscribe to it. Ignorance is no excuse. Notice how those living as indigenous people still live the same way now as they did thousands of years ago. There are those who will point out that many indigenous people did very cruel and unkind acts of violence. I am of the opinion they only became this way after the influence of Jehovah and His invading ways.

****

Only those who meditate know what they are talking about! Only those who do conscious Out Of Body Experiences know the nature of things from a conscious perspective.

And only those who meditate open-mindedly are accurate in what they experience and share. Those who are stuck within ancient traditions still live a misguided life. No two people are the same. No two people live according to the same truths as others. The oxymoron of human life is two or more people subscribing to the ideas of others under the guise of some tradition. Insanity is when two or more people live a tradition, like religion or science. No two grains of sand are the same. No two leaves are the same, or blades of grass, or snowflakes. Each shows us what infinity is. This is the same with people. No two are the same. Reality and truth differ from person to person. Universality and specific-ness make us self/ego. When a woman gives birth, why is each child different from anyone else within the same family of the same gender? Infinity is the answer, so why do so many live according to fictions that only had or have relevance to the one who experienced the ideas shared? Once a truth is realized it becomes. irrelevant to the next moment of now. It is only the ego that holds to the past as if it is what is now.

The art of propaganda is in how successful it is over time. The invader culture and all it stands for relies entirely upon the success of propaganda to thrive until it self-destructs. Even when this has occurred, every invader culture resurrects itself according to that ideal. This is akin to people experiencing disease and refusing to change what creates it within the body, which ends up living as the disease, rather than what and where disease can lead. Opposites lead to each other. This is true of everything. Within a medium that is infinite, everything has an opposite that balances it into what it is not as the expression it is. This is how individuality is made possible. The ego treats everything as an entity unto itself. When it is overly fearful, everything is considered a threat.

The warlord god Jehovah was the answered response to those He conquered. His enslavement is covenanted chosen-ness through religious dogma that reinforces fear, guilt, arrogance, and denial. The test of any idea is, does it make one feel negative or positive? What does an idea engender one to feel, think, and act upon?! Usually people feel pain, fear, or guilt, stemming from denial and karma. These are our responsibility to heal and end here. Few do, so the invader culture remains intact.

Money is one big Ponzi scheme. War is the ego conflicted with itself. Class distinction is humanness converted into an elitist arrogance of delusion. These are the great fictions Jehovah has contributed to humanity as the invader culture. Many sources now intuited by fools play on our frailties and gullibility. Few question the true intentions of their source and what aspect of the creation they serve. Again, individual sources are more negative than positive. Collective sources are more positive than negative. Individuality is more negative than positive by design. Our positive nature is our collectiveness. This is also true of humanity as a whole.

Invading the Indigenous while the Rest of Us Watch

The ego is very good at spouting the idea of oneness. What is the oneness of humanity? The Christ, when it lives the Love of Yahweh, Light of Id, love of mom, and light of dad. These four states make us human beings. As previously stated, this also can be thought of as: divinity as the heart, deity as the head, love as our feminine side, and light as our masculine side. There are an endless number of ways to understand who we are. Ideas are simply and merely tools used to assist us in our awareness and ability to live life honorably and authentically. The art of the invader culture is designed to keep us steeped in fear, guilt, arrogance, and denial about how we humanly portray God, planet, and universe as our self/ego. The majority of people on this planet do not realize they are being deliberately lied to by the faith they place in these fictions of the mind of those who support the invader culture as the way of life and God. Soon, these pretenders will be exposed.

The question we all have to ask ourselves is: "Why do we choose to believe false doctrine?" Anyone pointing a finger will only do so at him or herself. That is all we do in life. Life only mirrors back to us what we feel, sense, think, and envision is the way it is. Everyone is entitled to being and living exactly as he or she chooses to. Anyone who stipulates otherwise is a fool and is lying to us. God is all that is, including each one of us. We are each the image and likeness of God. Each of us states, as and through our life, the I Am-ness of God. Everything within the creation is God's I Am-ness. What we do unto anything, we do unto God. I do not see fit to kill what God saw fit to create! All life forms are entitled to theirs, as I am entitled to mine.

Eleven thousand years of Jehovistic Satanism's evil sin is coming to an abrupt end, taking billions with it. Those who leave will be convinced the world has ended, because there is no coming back for all who do not survive. Reincarnation will no longer be an option for those not left behind to continue our human evolution until it collectively ascends. Individual ascension is more negative than positive. This is true for all souls that have ascended as an entity unto itself. It is the nature of energy. The negative charge is individual, as the electron. The positive charge is the collective nature of energy. When balanced, these are neutral. Neutrality then develops through discipline into polarization at our level of existence. These determine path of service.

Some choose the negative path, while some choose the positive path. The role that the masters play is not for us to blindly follow them, like so many have done with Buddha and Jesus, or with the gurus and various nuns and monks; rather, it is our aspiring to live as conscious as they were as our reality and truth. This is something people just do not get. The invader culture is dead set against our knowing our true nature and purpose for existing humanly. Humanness is an abomination to Jehovah and the invader culture. This is why every indigenous culture was invaded and almost destroyed as the historicity of this planet. This is the legacy of the warlord god Jehovah and his chosen people, existing as every invader culture on this planet. War only exists against Yahweh's true design as the indigenous people.

When observing the invader, or the indigenous we see both aspects of human evolution at work, from the perspective of our lives as the arbitrary. As discussed earlier, Biblically, this is the Old Testament, the life of Jesus, and the theology of Paul. The Old Testament is living negatively. The life of Jesus is living positively. The theology of Paul is living arbitrarily. Christians have lumped all three into a form of religious insanity. Only the living dead die and go to heaven. Death is the ego getting even with itself. God created life, which is the eternality of love and light, lived as our embodied spirituality. When we all decide to live, rather than die, we all will ascend as what is eternal, as the Christ. This is collective ascension.

This is something science and religion do not want whatsoever. Human evolution begins when the invader culture becomes extinct. Evolution is what the created does after it becomes a living life form. Essential to the invader culture way of existing is creating conflict between points of view. This is why there is division within every tradition. Conflict ensures that peace and harmony will never exist even though these are the natural ways of life and existence. The

Invading the Indigenous while the Rest of Us Watch

primary belief held by the dying, good versus evil, predominates every aspect of our lives within the invader culture mindset. This is not natural to our existence or to the creation.

I can count on either hand the number of friends I have out of seven billion people. It is this way for most of us. We are unfriendly. Then, we wonder why we are left alone by the rest of the universe. We wonder why Yahweh and Id leave us alone. We are left alone by what created us and brought us to life, because knowledge of Yahweh and Id has been completely removed from our awareness, so from our point of existence, they do not exist. Earth, in all its beauty and majesty, is a human ghetto due to the influences catering to the invader culture mindset within the lives of people and to the various sources the ignorant allow to use them in order to maintain negativity as an predominance on this planet. This makes the channel a culprit of perpetuation. This is also the karma of everyone who subscribes to any way of life that is foreign and contrary to our design and our way of being/living.

My role in life is only that of human being-ness, and all it entails. I have walked the path of the master-less seeker. My knowing has come through experience. I have read lots, and lots, and lots of books. I have understood most ideas instantly. Some ideas have taken me years to understand. Experience is the only measure whereby realness and truth have any relevance. Sharing expanded awareness is the only purpose wisdom serves. Being true to one's reality and truth is the only that works, humanly. Sacrifice and martyrdom are what one does when he or she lives according to the ideas of others through a tradition that has ancient roots. Sacrifice and martyrdom in all forms is suicide. Death is a form of suicide that requires reincarnation to heal.
way

Identification leads to idol worship and self-glorification when the ego remains unresolved. Death is the result of our only paying attention to our bodies, the ego, and all things out there. Our attention is continuously drawn to outer-based sources. We are dazzled by technology. We love being entertained by the foolishness of others. We unconsciously choose to deny and ignore God and universe as our life, humanly existing on this planet. God and universe are relegated to quantum physics and astronomy through denial, projection, and objectification.

Religion has only accomplished one thing about God. It teaches us false doctrine about us as God's image and likeness. Thousands of false gods are worshipped religiously. Religion only exists as it does to replace the reality of Yahweh and the truth of Id for ideologies of various gods that do not exist or pertain to our life as the image and likeness of God according to the love of Yahweh and light of Id. Graven images stand as the ideals we aspire to through the ego. It is interesting that Christianity focuses upon the crucifixion of Jesus rather than upon any other aspect of his life and teaching. Not surprisingly, this identification is the single most important element within the theological dogma of that faith. Why Jesus chose this to be as part of his life experience is curious. I suspect it was a mistake on his part. Also interesting was his statement, "Forgive them, Father, for they know not what they do." What was it about his life that he did not understand about forgiveness until he was on the cross? Jesus is just another graven image worshipped by those who are afraid, in denial, and guilt ridden. This is true of all externally based images. (I am curious as to what will end Catholicism as a religion practiced by almost one billion people.) Curious also that Jesus taught forgiveness, rather than acceptance, for love is accepting of everything and everyone as it is or they are regardless of how reprehensible or unlovable something or someone is.

Invading the Indigenous while the Rest of Us Watch

Negativity and Our True Identity

Negativity is the basis for infinity and individuality. Lacking this aspect of energy, God's I Am-ness would not be possible. Converting negativity into an absolute is the self-serving role. For us, it is the ego. Many a false prophet clamors about. Many make the mistake of becoming spiritual prostitutes by selling their gifts to others. Gifts from God are freely given to us, and it is wise to freely share them with others. Money is a trap many do not evolve beyond. It is the golden calf of the invader culture's insanity. Bartering is more evolved than financial exchange. Economics based upon money always leads to depression. Personally, money is a form of debt consciousness. Control is the reason debt takes place. Those who are owed through debt control others. This is how great nations collapse. Money is just a game played by those who are greedy. Greed is balanced by poverty. Ending poverty requires the elimination of greed as a point of view.

Ending the invader culture requires our returning to living as designed. To do so requires each of us becoming conscious of whom we are as the image and likeness of God. Not easy to accomplish, as there are so many versions of how we came into existence. Darwin stated we evolved from apes. Science tells us we evolved from nothing through chance occurrences happening over billions of years. Christianity tells us we were created by God and are its image and likeness, and that we were created from the dust of the ground as Adam and Eve. Edgar Cayce stated that seven root races were created simultaneously. According to the Council of Layett, Yahweh created us and Id brought us to life 75,000 years ago. That time frame is also documented in the RA Material/Law of One.

The universe is the 'Word' of God. This planet is the 'Word' of God. Our life is the 'Word of God. Not surprisingly, the egos of some changed these ideas into a book being the 'Word of God, called the Bible. The Greek word is logos, which means universe, but can also be translated into word. It is only our stuck-ness that blinds us to so-called holy works that are thousands of years old. Only the ego holds to and believes in ideas that are based in the past, maintained presently, and continue on as our future. What is completely missed by the ego is the self- sustaining, self-regenerating, and self-perpetuating through the instantaneous, spontaneous, and simultaneous as the now, here, being. The ego, as an outer point of view, is only interested in what it can get from external sources. This is all and only what it believes in as the outer aspect of who we are.

Again, the race is on as to what actually destroys this planet, pollution or nuclear warheads. That is the goal of the invader culture-destroying God, life, humanness, and all else, one planet at a time. If allowed to do so, every invader culture would destroy the universe. The path of the person living the invader way of death is pain,. fear, anger, hatred, and violence. These are acted out by many daily. Children watch cartoons that are very violent. Young adults play video games consisting of war, gang violence, and various forms of conflict between good and evil. We consider violence a means to an end. There is the belief that sacrificing the lives of some for the many eventually brings about peace. The self-perpetuating teaches us otherwise. Anything we live by remains as-is until we change what we feel and think about it. This requires our examining every belief held, especially those forming science and religion. People need to get back to living their imagination and using it creatively to manifest a life that is positive and based upon love and light. Hollywood has the audacity of filming the notion that true love always and only leads to tragedy and death. Love is eternal and never dies! The ego is 'fear felt' that dies, taking the body with it when it goes. The body is held hostage by the ego that is fear given a face many wear to the grave.

The invader culture is negativity lived socially. Socialism is the great nemesis for every invader culture, as it eliminates class distinction. Capitalism and communism are basically the

Invading the Indigenous while the Rest of Us Watch

same ideology. What communism does politically, capitalism does economically. How does humanity end the invader culture way of life? By eliminating everything involved with war, greed, and class distinction. By eliminating those traditional institutions based upon false doctrine and forms of propaganda. Propaganda is anything believed in that does not come through one's intuition. All forms of outer-based information are types of propaganda, even this book you now are reading. All true teachings and teachers will lead the seeker to looking within and listening, We are even taught that, "the kingdom of the father is within." "Within the quietude of silence rests the voice of God."

The invader culture convinces us that only 'out there' exist. It also has us believing that 'out there' is deadly-that it is to be feared above all else. Humanity is conned into believing fear is real and very violent. People perceive life as life threatening. Everything and everyone is to be feared. Self-serving individuals, acting as false gods and prophets, come along, promising to protect us from our unresolved fears. All we have to do is give our power away by relying on their propaganda as 'the' truth and as the way for us to be delivered from evils self-imagined.

Pitiful people come, guilt ridden, hoping to convince us that their way of helplessness is the human condition. Puffed up egos bellow about obeying God to avoid eternal damnation and living a cursed life. All I say is, "Give God a rest, and shut the heck up!" Perpetrators only exist due to our unresolved karma and our belief that we are helpless. Perpetrators reincarnate as the exact victim, according to what they perpetrated. This is the law of karma, which is why Buddha taught, "Do not do unto others what you do not want done unto you." Which is why Jesus taught, "Do unto others as you would have them do unto you." Which is why I teach, "You only do to others what you are doing to yourself."

Myopia is the viewpoint of the ego. It never takes very much into consideration. The ego is the 6 to 10 percent of the brain that is active. The other 90 to 94 percent involves and pertains to our mind, body, spirit, and soul. Opening the heart and activating the brain are part of our path. Living love, as our body, and light, as our spirituality, is also part of our responsibility. Understanding and utilizing God's will is another choice we can make. Becoming fully conscious is also our responsibility. People pray to nonexistent entities, hoping they will do for us what we are unwilling to do for ourselves. The day will come when all the entities assisting us will leave us alone, so that we will be forced to become responsible for our lives. This will require us all to pay attention to what we feel, sense, think, and envision about our life and the reasons why we believe what we do about existence. Oil will be withdrawn forcing us to take responsibility for our lives. People actually believe that the warlord god Jehovah is "our one true God."

After all, it's in the Bible, and the Bible is the "Word of God." Nonsense that is presented as dogmatic belief is next to impossible to reason with. Religious conviction blinds all who subscribe to the points of fictions revered as the truth. Reward and punishment are the promises made by ideologies whose sole intention is taking the believer to the grave after having given hiser power away by placing hiser faith in the false doctrine. The art of the invader culture is how successful it is in getting people to believe, generation after generation, ideas that are not based upon anything real or true. Science has accomplished this, as has religion. Education also does its part in deluding people.

How many people will be left behind after the final battle between Jehovah and Id? I suspect it will be about seven tenths of 1 percent of seven billion people- that's roughly forty-nine million people. Almost all of those living indigenously will be left behind. Those people who choose to be love and know light as hiser embodied spirituality shared kindly and generously will also be left behind. Everyone who clings to hiser fear, guilt, arrogance, and denial will not make the grade. Those who think they will disappear, vanishing into thin air, are in for a very rude awakening. Most of humanity will have its eyes opened very soon. Many will clamor about, accusing whomever of having lied to them through every outer- based source believed in. This is inevitable given the nature and role of the ego

Invading the Indigenous while the Rest of Us Watch

and how most only choose to live as and according to that mask. The ego, as our outer sense of identity, only believes in and relates to external sources.

Great teachers come to educate and deliver humanity from fear and arrogance. They have been and are universally rejected, denied, ignored, and denigrated by egotists and misguided malcontents only interested in fitting in and maintaining the invader culture and all it entails. The 'holy war' rages on. Greed remains unmitigated. Class distinction glorifies the ego of many who discover after death that their karma requires lifetimes to heal. We are responsible for all the lives of others we affected humanly. After death, everyone is shown hiser life, and karma is addressed. Anything negative affecting others requires atonement. Atonement is how negativity is balanced through experience. This requires reincarnation to accomplish. Death and reincarnation remain our legacy until we eventually get it about ascension and move on.

Ascension means rising above, taking with, and integrating into. What we rise above are all lower forms of consciousness, like what we die for currently. What we take with us is our body, for the body is only love made into an image that gives God identity humanly. What we integrate into is the larger community of universe when love and light are lived as our humanity. This requires God, planet, and universe lived as one's life consciously. Owning the awareness of mind, body, spirit, and soul precedes one's actual ascension. The mind is God that is personal. The body is love lived personally. The spirit is light lived personally. The soul is the consciousness of all that is, owned as one's infinitude/universality. These four states are unified into a state of oneness. They are the perfection of our humanity. Humanness is the unified field theory.

What prevents us all from being and knowing our true identity is gender disparity. This is like stating the right hemisphere of the brain is greater and superior to the left side, or that the head is superior to the heart. Insanity is believing nonsense as if it were fact. Most of humanity is insane for believing much of what it does- especially when lives are taken because people choose to disagree with fictions, figments, and what is untrue. How is taking the life of another an act of love? How does the commandment "Thou shalt not kill" come into play when people choose to take another's life? How do Christians reconcile that commandment when engaged in war?

Arbitrariness is curious in how it works for 'true believers.' One day, the truth is this, and then the next day, it is the opposite. Anyone reading the Bible from cover to cover will discover exact opposites within its pages. These are ignored. The fact is, Jesus taught love to resolve fear, forgiveness to resolve judgment, and doing unto others to resolve persecution. Fear is the way of the Old Testament. Love was the life of Jesus. Arbitrariness was the theology of Paul. People choose to live as the negative, the positive, or the arbitrary. Confusion is not easy to resolve when people are convinced they are correct in their insanity. Change is constant, and nothing changes for us humanly, even when the ridiculous is obvious. It is curious how nations evolve into greatness, only to make the same mistakes of failure every fallen nation has made century after century. This is the way of the invader culture. War, greed, and class distinction are essentially negative and arbitrary through the fear and arrogance that gives rise to them. These remain unchanged until they become extinct.

Invading the Indigenous while the Rest of Us Watch

What the Invader Culture Does Not Tell You

Humanity is living like the dinosaurs right before they became extinct. Extinction is the un-viability of an organism within a medium that changes beyond the parameters of continued existence. This is how energy works according to what evolves along with it. This requires a connected integration with the parameters of energy as it evolves into a greater, more comprehensive state of existence. This requires people understanding not only what energy is humanly, but also how it works with regards to density. According to the RA Material/Law of One, there are seven densities composing the universe, each with eight octaves, like musical scales. There are two other states, presence and Godhood, which precede the creation and exist after the creation. How I understand all nine states is: presence, is-ness, realness, pattern, content, truth, I am-ness, all-ness, and Godhood. Two through eight correspond to the seven charkas. These all arise out of God's original state of existence-what I call all encompassing-ness that surrounds the universe.

It is essential to one's existence to understand inner being-ness and how it becomes an outer manifestation as the body and the environment. Fundamental to this is God's will to be and know. This is how the universe came into existence. God willed Itself into expression infinitely. We do the same process as our experiences-- we will/intend into expression our entire human drama. The mind creates the body. The spirit brings this to life. The soul incarnates into the body and becomes conscious of itself as a human being that knows, shares, and ascends. This is accomplished through extension and expansion of what is intended.

Douglas H. Melloy

Faith is the evidence of things unseen. Desire develops one's faith. Intention is the fulfillment of what one's faith and desire is focused on. This can be anything at all. "Nothing is inappropriate given one's measure of the world," writes Neale Donald Walsch in Conversations With God. What an astute statement. Experience as expressed is why creation exists for everything. Everything is an aspect of God. Everything images God. What we do to a given aspect of life here on Earth, we do unto God. How we interact with others and this planet is how we treat God. Again, when Jesus stated, "Unto the least of these, ye do unto Me," what he was actually saying was, anything you do, you do unto God.

This is what the invader culture just does not get. Selfishness only cares about itself. It seeks to be glorified and catered to unceasingly. I call this the syndrome of the king and queen. It is the ego puffed up and catered to nonstop. Money, fame, and power are the basis for what is considered successful by almost everyone- even though these have little significance to creation. Everything acquired possession-wise is left behind. What is taken with one is what's real and true that one learned through experience. Ultimately, what is learned is how creativity works so that it is conducive to one's life and the larger community of the planet. This is then utilized within the larger community of the universe. Making a contribution is all we actually learn to contribute to God's infinite being-ness. When the contribution made is universal by nature, ascension is possible. This requires one to understand will, love, light, and consciousness as one's being-ness shared. Few accomplish this effectively.

Most of humanity only accomplishes following the dictates as stipulated by a given ideal established by the invader culture through tradition that is never questioned or evolved beyond. People play the same game generation after generation. Ascension is only possible when humanness is lived at a universal and infinite level of being. The invader culture intention makes this impossible to accomplish. Death, after suffering, becomes the only options available to those who have become enslaved to the invader way of dying. This is sacrificing God's image for an ideology that is only interested in

Invading the Indigenous while the Rest of Us Watch

death and destruction. Everyone who has died has agreed that the invader way is 'it,' not God, life, humanness, and ongoing-ness.

Again, what the invader culture cultivates is people becoming robots, zombies, and puppets. Controlled manipulation is the art of the invader culture. People are brainwashed into only following the rules established, never feeling anything real, and allowing those in power to get them to do whatever. Allurements carrot the unsuspecting into doing reprehensible acts under the guise that it is for the common good of business, politics, or some other organization. People never question the effects of application on the well being of others and the environment. Anything we do, we do to ourselves. This is karma.

The West is very good at fooling itself into thinking it can do whatever and get away with it. The idea of karma is unnecessary when one lives an honorable and authentic life, where compassion and kindness are what are felt and shared. The only usefulness of understanding through experience is when what one feels and thinks that is real and true is shared through one's life with others. This is the measure by which one's life is graded. Ascension is graduating into a life that continues to contribute at a greater level of being. Useful conduciveness is the only thing that matters to creation. Respect and reverence are the means by which one will ascend after service is provided.

Knowing the self/ego and serving others culminates in ascension, again with positive ascension being collective ascension and individual ascension being more negative than positive. The positive nature of the self is its collectiveness. The ego is the negative, and only thinks of itself in terms of existing as a body separated from all else. The soul is self-aware of itself as human. The body is what feels the effects of both the positive and the negative. This is so energy composed of both will be understood as what it is as one's life, humanly. Then one will know how the positive and the negative affect others, life on this planet, and the planet itself. Only when one becomes effective in hiser applications is ascension possible. Karma teaches us this. Karma is our experiencing of both positive and negative applications through various lifetimes. All anyone learns is feeling something real and thinking something true, which are shared in ways that are kind and conducive. This is the measure by which one stands or falls.

This is also true of nations. They are the larger body of humanity. This is called the Christ when people choose to consciously live love and light as a collective. When people resolve their ego, they evolve into a collective state of being and knowing. The natural tendency is sharing this with others. When enough people live this, collective ascension is made possible. The invader culture is only interested in teaching people how to be assassins. Its sole emphasis is on finding people who are willing to become ruthless, people who are willing to sacrifice everything and everyone just to empower themselves. Those who will do whatever it takes to get ahead are then selected out of the masses for more ruthless activities. Ultimately, war, greed, and class distinction are established as the power bases for those who are ruthless. These are how the invader culture operates. Those truly successful are usually worshipped as gods among the living.

These types of individuals are the basis for every false god worshipped by people. The ego only knows how to identify with what it seeks to become, a false god worshipped by many. The invader culture exists so that the ego will become a false god. This is no different than what the warlord god Jehovah is and created as the invader culture on this planet. Jehovah is like a super ego at war with the entire creation. Jehovah is "the one true God" of Judaism and Christianity. This entity is to the universe what Hitler was to Germany. It is this god that returns to destroy those enslaved to its self-serving ways, only because the unsuspecting do not realize what Jehovah is and does with people and planets-through the ideology and psychology that establishes the invader culture according to traditions existing as institutions.

This requires division, competition, disparity, conflict, dysfunction, confusion, and destructiveness to work. Chaos theory is the only one that makes any sense. Systems theories abound, positing nonsense ideas people believe are the way it is. Violence is the art and way of the self-serving, ensuring that the invader culture remains intact so that Jehovah will return to finish what began as conquering, this continues through enslavement, and will end the world of all who support way of death. This is the way of the ego for everyone. It is accomplished through the art of destroying, what was conquered and enslaved through ideology disseminated long ago.

    Death is only possible when one is addicted to and distracted by it through fear and arrogance. These doom the aspirant into dying and going to heaven. The invader culture mindset is masterful at playing on one's fears and catering to one's arrogance, so that war, greed, and class distinction remain the way it is for humanity. The invader culture only lasts until the return of that which introduced it to a given planet. In our case, it is the warlord god Jehovah, recorded in the religions of Judaism and Christianity. Everyone who practices these two religions is responsible for why Jehovah returns. Jehovah returns because people are more interested in death and destruction than in peace and harmony. It is like Jehovah comes to destroy what God created, because humanity wants that more than life itself.

    Personal and social affliction is only possible through people feeling that way about themselves and life. Healing is only possible through letting go, after understanding what's involved with what afflicts us and all the dramas we face. That is why the idea exists that we create our reality. This way, we can own up and accept that we are responsible for what we feel, sense, think, and envision is our life and reality. When who we are makes sense, and pertains to what is, then our life corresponds to the reality as a personal truth. The dogma of blanket ideas covering vast things does not make any sense, especially when two or more people are involved. Reality is self-defined by each of us through our existence and exposed to us through experience, which reveals to us what we actually feel and think is our life. Ideas only have relevance to the person who feels that hiser life is that way. Reality differs from person to person, as and at this level of egotistical existence. It is this and everything else. Infinity is and means all things are possible and, by thought, exist. This is true of any idea felt to be. The ego and self' are the choice we make as to how we exist humanly. We decide which is our reality. Then we seek to polarize either one into what evolves.

Propaganda denies everything. Its role is making sure false doctrine is revered as sacred truth. False doctrine is the premise of the invader culture. Great traditions stand through institutions that only exist to keep the invader culture alive and thriving until it becomes extinct. The success of this way of death is in how many people it takes with it when it fades forever. For humanity, it is 99.3 percent because many people believe in and support this type of negativity. Each one of us chooses what we believe. Why that is so is personal and evolutionary. Discernment is not encouraged. Questioning is punishable by violence and death. The arrogant state, "Because I say so." People are lazy, so nothing changes in their life.

People want to be believed by peers, so a lot of information is written just towards that end. Never mind if what is stated is pure fiction. Never mind if what is documented is done in order that people believe nonsense disguised through religion, or science, or some other self-serving propaganda. So many enticements can be very alluring. So many figments sound so true. The invader cultures existing today are very sophisticated. They maintain war, greed, and class distinction as God's way. Successful wars last for decades. Money remains the single most important thing for almost everyone. Class distinction is the aspiration of the majority of people. None of these ideals is why the universe exists. Why do so many people place their faith in ideologies that are so contrary to our design?

The end times come only because people believed in and placed their faith in what self-destructs eventually. Our death experience is no different than this, humanly. It is, on a personal level, what the end times are on a social and global level. We fail to get this, so we die. Death is the success of ideas believed in that cause this for everyone whose life passes on. We console ourselves through the belief we will go to a better place than this--that up there is perfect and down here is tragic and vicious. People allow the

Invading the Indigenous while the Rest of Us Watch

attitudes of others to persuade them to cater to insane nonsense and reprehensible deeds. It seems our ethics and morality are lacking,

Ideas are fine when based on experiences that correspond to states that are real and true. This requires people to aspire to living ideals that are ongoing and conducive to humanness and to what has the capability of continued existence. The role people like me play is that we are the essence of being what is real and true humanly. Our humanity is the humanity that exists. This is what will ascend after service is contributed to others humbly and transparently. Human potential has the ability to live for hundreds of years. Most people do not because they hold to their ego so strongly. The ego denies the existence of God and universe as the natures of the self. The ego denies life. It fears all that is. Again, death is the ego getting even with itself.

****

The choices we make humanly are either: pain, fear, darkness, and negativity; or joy, love, light, and the positive, as our death or life experiences. Some are convinced evil exists, so petty tyrants come to save us from ourselves and our fearful beliefs. Many a wolf in sheep's clothing comes offering us hope and eternal salvation. They only accomplish taking our energy, money, and life. Great egos bellow. We bow down. They bank. We struggle. Then, the nonphysical aspect of creation arranges energy so that we feel at home according to our imagined reference of this state. It will be whatever we think it is. Infinity means that anything/everything is possible as a point of view, reference, or experience.

The ego is absolutist in its idolatry. Many a puffed up one parades about like a charade. Many bow down to the ego of others. The ego insists upon making fellow souls into graven images, like we have done with Buddha and Jesus. The ego denigrates God's image into fallen-ness and 'sin.' We are guilty just being alive. To Jehovah, humanness is an abomination. It is completely contrary to what Jehovah is and represents. The sad irony is that this is the kind of god the Jews and Christians worship as their "one true God." Paganism is a blanket term for anyone who lives a philosophy based upon what is real and true that corresponds to what created us and brought us to life. Few question why the term 'our' is used in the first chapter of Genesis, describing our creation. Yahweh and Id are our true gods that created us and brought us to life, making us the humanness of God on this planet using the Lemur as our blueprint. (RA Material/Law of One.)

People are entitled to live any way they see fit. Differences exist because of infinity. This is not only true of people, but of all the various life forms populating this planet. Everything is God's I Am-ness. Everything. I choose to allow, accept, acknowledge, and appreciate even-mindedly, or I fear, judge, and persecute others and the life on this planet. Our lives are measured by how positive or negative we are, humanly. People live indifferently, negatively, positively, or purposefully. Mindful purposefulness, embodied spirituality, and conscious awareness require discipline and the willingness to be humanness as a way of life. These are not easy to live. The ego is only interested in fitting in and being very, very busy.

The invader culture does everything it can to make sure that no one lives our design. Those who do are tortured and then put to death, like Jesus was. The irony is that we do this to ourselves through disease and the death experience. That is how successful the invader culture is and all those who subscribe to it. Sickness and disease are maintained through the medical profession. Doctors tell us we are diseased and that only medicine will save us by maintaining the disease. That is the only purpose doctors serve us. They maintain disease and death as the way it is for us humanly.
Disease exists through what is felt and thought within the mind, so that disease can be healed by changing what is felt and thought into what the disease is not, which is health and happiness through love and acceptance. That is the only purpose disease serves us. If doctors were actually involved with the act of healing, all diseases would be healed through them. The fact that they are not shows us that doctors are only interested in our sicknesses so they can

Invading the Indigenous while the Rest of Us Watch

make their millions and billions. Greed is the only reason why universal health care does not exist in America, like it does in Cuba, Canada, England, Australia, and France. Disease and sickness are states of one's mind. They are created by the mind through God's will. It is only one's fear that causes the person to rely on doctors and medicine. Medicine in any form is just a placebo for the ego. Anyone can change hiser mind about hiser condition, and it will change. This is true of anything that afflicts the body. It is only a state of mind. The mind creates anything felt as one's life. Many are enabled through the ignorance of others and doctors. It is a conflict of interest if a doctor makes money on any medicine prescribed. (I am fortunate I have never taken any medication for anything, not even aspirin.)

The invader culture insists there is nothing we can do about anything, that we are helpless to our own creativity. The art of controlled manipulation works very well in enslaving creativity that becomes manifested. The universe only shows us how and what creativity is as a manifestation of God. The universe is God given uniqueness. It gives God individuality and specific-ness. It makes God infinite and allows God to experience I Am-ness within everything composing the universe. It is the exploration of being and knowing through experience and understanding. (One is wise to be wary of any ideology that claims to be 'the' one or 'it.') I was married to a woman who went from Catholicism, to Nichiren Shoshu Buddhism, and then to Eckankar. Each tradition claims to be 'the' one. This is what negativity does as an absolute.

Experiences teach us about who we are and why we are here. They lead us where they do within the journey of self/ego. Esoterics are fine, but we are also human, so anything with which we are involved must involve our humanity. People often deny their humanness for ideals that are pointless, lacking the human elements. Humanness images God when it is lived as love and light. Love is the physical. Light is the spiritual. Combined, they make us human beings that know. When love and light are lived as an embodied spirituality, then ascension is possible. It is only our lacking these as our life that causes the death experience for us. The ego denies love and light as the body and spirit. The ego holds onto fear through denial and self-doubt. This ensures one will die.

Death and destruction are the ways of the invader culture and its false doctrines of deceit. Onward humanity marches to its doom. Humanity has refused to heal war as its basic way of life. It has refused to end money as a form of greed and spiritual prostitution. It has glorified the ego as a god. It has segregated people into elitist clans of contention and disrespect. Vanity and self-glorification fool many. False idols exist by the thousands. Yahweh and Id remain unknown to almost all humans.

The number thirteen is considered something very negative. Hollywood has made 13 into a horror story. Many fear this number. Some refuse to use it as part of their business. The number thirteen corresponds to the number of beings composing Yahweh, our creator. Jehovah hates Yahweh, and its creation of us as its contribution to God's infinitude.

Humanity is comfortably numb in its blind obedience and conformity. Arbitrariness is the way of most of humanity. The Paulists carry their crucifixes, showing the rest of humanity how they feel life is--as only forms of suffering and death. Everyone is expected to conform. Those who do not are condemned to eternal fire. Does that make any sense? Absolutely not, so why do people feel that way about themselves? It is because we are intolerant of our humanity through placing our faith in a warlord god that only seeks our death and destruction. Jehovah comes to play that role for everyone who believes that way. Jehovah comes for everyone who feels they deserve to be judged and destroyed. Nonbelievers will be spared, as they have no tie to Jehovah and his fulfilling of this death wish of destruction. Faith will bestow this upon every 'true believer.' It will be those who believe this idea of judgment that will experience it, not those who disbelieve.

Hierarchical ideologies of arrogance are why wars are fought. Elitism breeds contempt and hatred. Superiority instills the need for defeating others through acts of aggression. Competition is the

Invading the Indigenous while the Rest of Us Watch

attitude and behavior of the elitist ideal of superiority. Conflict only exists through the ideology of good versus evil. The ego is good, so God and universe are evil. Believing these has made us insane and inhumane. So, we build robots and clone things, thinking we can do a better job than God in what we create as versions of our ego.

Humanity has lost itself with its technology. Technology always fails those who become dependant upon it for survival, due in part because of the addictive nature of the ego. People have not figured out the differences between living naturally versus artificially. Some are convinced they can replace that which is God with manmade artifacts. It is puzzling that the destructive is allowed to destroy entire planets. Asteroids are the remains of planets destroyed by entities, like Jehovah. Negative and positive service polarity is not understood by very many, so both play their charades until the negative is no longer an active agency for people. The path is how one comes to choose what he or she will serve as hiser life purpose.

People do not resolve the fiction of opposites in conflict. The ego projects these into God the good and Satan/Devil the bad. Conflict is impossible within a medium that is one state, which is the universe. The oneness of God is confused with "the one true God." People do not examine many of the ideas composing traditions. Many religious ideas maintain the arts of war, greed, and class distinction. These are contrary to our fundamental and basic natures. No one questions the absurdity of many ideas being believed as the way it is-as God's way. To such an extent, nothing changes, humanly. Humanity has not evolved very far in eleven thousand
years.

Man's inhumanity to man remains unchanged. People refuse to apply themselves to love and wisdom as the arts of appropriateness. The best we do is to incur karma, so that we have to reincarnate over and over to heal it. Anything perpetrated by us has to be our experienced victimization done in another lifetime. This is the law of reciprocity. It is taught as "do unto others, for what you do unto others is actually done unto yourself." Karma is ignored here in the West. Anything goes, and we fail to get it about consequences for everything we feel and think. These two aspects of being are misunderstood, humanly. The processes of extension and expansion of energy are not grasped by many. If people realized that every experience is based upon feeling and thinking, most would pay attention to their emotions and their thoughts.

These become the belief systems we implement and admire. Ideas are curious, as is the imagination. Many assume that what they feel and think has nothing to do with God, planet, and universe. This is never the case. Every idea felt affects everything else due to connected integration. Everything existing within the creation is connected to everything by design. It is only our sense of isolation that convinces us otherwise through the catalyst of pain. Pain convinces us we have separated from source as the birth experience. Fear convinces us we are isolated from all else. Darkness convinces us we are distanced from everything, Negativity convinces us we are at odds with everything. Some believe chaos gives rise to organization. What we end up with is mass confusion, coupled with the attitude that anything goes.

Each of us is given the liberty of living as we choose to through God's will to be and know humanly, according to our soul's blueprint. This is something many do not understand. The blueprint of the soul is determined before one incarnates. Then, experiences correspond to what the soul's purpose is for incarnating. This comes down to experience and karma. Experience is the only way something is lived. Karma is the only way acts of selfishness are understood, through experiencing the act as a victim of it. Many might think twice about what they contribute to others when that which is shared is cruel or unkind.

"Nothing is inappropriate given one's measure of the world." This is what God tells Neale Donald Walsch in Conversations With God. Much of what we observe are forms of insanity. Only the insane participate in war, greed, and class distinction. Death is also a form of insanity. Outside and beyond the moment of experience, ideas are irrelevant and pointless. Yet, we insist upon holding onto

Invading the Indigenous while the Rest of Us Watch

ideas for thousands of years, through institutionalized traditions. Just because one billion people believe in a tradition does not make it correct or true. It is not intended for us to follow sheepishly the ideas of another even when the one followed was enlightened. It is our responsibility to become as conscious as anyone else. This requires being and knowing what God, planet, and universe are, as our self/ego existing as our humanness.

The requirements for the success of false doctrines are fear, guilt, arrogance, and denial of what makes us human beings. This is the basis of the invader culture, with its emphasis upon war, money, and the idea that some people are superior to others. Remember, within a medium that is infinite, nothing has greater or lesser value than anything else. Value given to something is strictly the choice of someone establishing what that is. This is also true of meaning. Each of us gives the only meaning something has through interpretation. This is the basis for what we feel and think through reinforcement. The ego has to be right at the cost of life itself! Death is only a belief system that most revere. This is also true of disease and conflict.

Energy conforms itself to willed intention. This will be anything experienced within one's life. God's will creates every experience, according to desire, purpose, karma, and interest. Contrasted against this is a hidden agenda within one's life, and the essence of traditions and what is taught to us. Many do not question or seek to discern the agendas of what exists as science and religion or as the other main ideologies governing most societies. Few question the belief in good versus evil, so war remains constant as a social behavior. People believe in the idea of survival of the fittest. What is lacking is our realizing the difference between "taking possession of" and "being in possession of." What we are in possession of is the will of God, love of the creator, light of the bestower, and the consciousness of all that is. These exist as us-as our mind, body, spirit, and soul. They are the humanness of God, life, identity, and awareness.

Douglas H. Melloy

Part II:

The Indigenous Way of Life

Invading the Indigenous while the Rest of Us Watch

Original Design

I am of the opinion that the indigenous are our original design. That every indigenous race on this planet is how we were created to live as humanly. Many balk at this idea, but I know it is true. I am also of the opinion that bartering is more evolved than financial exchange. So, how did humanity get lost in its portrayal of God humanly? Look no farther than all the ideas composing the invader culture. This has led most of humanity astray. Living indigenously requires actualizing one's biology as it exists. Few do this today. Much of what composes the invader culture is versions of the golden calf. Life is intended to be lived simply and carefree. When we examine our life, we find that our heart corresponds to God, our body to this planet, our head to the four phases of the moon, and our consciousness to all that is, i.e., the universe, or that which is infinite.

It is not surprising that every invader culture has almost succeeded in exterminating every indigenous people from the surface of this planet through disease and warfare. This is by intention. The removal of every aspect pertaining to and involving Yahweh and Id has been very successful. It is as if they do not exist and have never existed. This is the role that way of life plays. The indigenous represent the human ideal as intended by Yahweh and Id. The intention of the warlord god Jehovah is destroying humanness completely by replacing that which is the image and likeness of God with ideologies that are foreign and contrary to our basic and true nature. Very successful are all the ideologies utilized that conquer, enslave, and destroy God's humanness. The unsuspecting do not realize how subtle and pervasive false doctrine is, as used by every invader culture. "The first shall be last, and the last shall be first,"

Douglas H. Melloy

bears this out as it refers to indigenous people. They were the first people and they will return to being the first people.

Most of humanity watches both cultures living according to their respective ideologies. Few realize what is actually going on and why. One clue that is useful is, how does each way of life treat the planet? Invader cultures seek to destroy the planet through pollution and bombs, while the indigenous live harmoniously with the environment. The indigenous treat the planet with reverence and respect, while invader cultures seek to conquer nature by enslaving it and then destroying it. It has almost succeeded in doing just that

Every indigenous culture has been decimated to the brink of extinction by invader cultures. This is accomplished through hatred and arrogance towards what Yahweh and Id created and brought to life 75,000 years ago. This is according to the RA Material/Law of One. Most of humanity does not realize this today. Most believe all sorts of nonsense disguised as truth and fact. Facts are fictions realized years too late. The propaganda of proof fools many. Nothing is provable within the constancy of change, yet many are convinced something can be proven. Ironic it is that people come into a knowing that is then demonstrated as a machine. Nothing in the universe is fixed or permanent, yet we act as if that is the case. We treat and consider all of existence as mechanistic. Machines are our great legacy, not living our biology as the image and likeness of God.

Living humanly requires embracing and owning our life according to what makes us such. This can be thought of as sun, earth, moon, and universe, or as that which radiates, absorbs, illuminates, and encompasses. A good field of study is comparing how invaders and indigenous live planet-wise. Invaders live according to false doctrine entirely, while the indigenous live authentically when living as intended. It is very easy for people to get sidetracked by ideas that are more fiction than truth. Everyone has hiser ideology that he or she subscribes to. Many only seek for what reinforces their point of view or reference for being. Discernment is not easy given the pervasiveness of many ideas. Every outer- based ideology seeks to accomplish one agenda-convincing people a particular

Invading the Indigenous while the Rest of Us Watch

propaganda is believed by as many as possible. The truer one's life, the less likely it is that people will listen and evolve. Few listened and believed in what Buddha knew as his life, while he was living. Now, a billion people place their faith in an ideology that is lacking much. True also for the two billion people who practice Christianity as their dogma of faith.

The denial of God as one's life usually leads to projection as something objectified. People worship all kinds of egotistical images. They are nothing more than graven images. The original state and condition of God is all encompassing, which the universe exists within. This state is uniform and constant. The universe is this state diversified into an infinitude. Everything that exists within the universe is the I Am-ness of God. Everything.

As previously stated, every aspect of the creation corresponds to three states of existence or being. They are the positive, the negative, and the neutral or. arbitrary. Invader cultures are negative, the indigenous are positive, and those who live arbitrarily are neutral. Each of us chooses what to feel, think, and act according to these three states of energy. The positive and negative are balanced as the neutral. The path leading to purpose is that aspect of energy, positive or negative, that is the most attractive to us. Then, we aspire to live as either someone who serves him or her self or others. These are the right and left hands of God. Choosing service polarity is human evolution. Only these are what evolve humanly. Lacking polarity, personal and social evolution is impossible. What we observe with both cultures is a lack of real and actual evolution. What we evolve beyond are all the limitations inherent in both ways of life.

When people live both positive and negative ideas, this cancels each into what does not evolve. What is useful is doing a positive/negative meditation. Breathe in the positive and exhale its opposite or negative quality. Then allow the wisdom to come so that the negative is understood. Do this for as long as it takes so that energy is completely understood as your life at this level of existence. I practiced this meditation for twenty years.

Douglas H. Melloy

****

Good versus evil requires hatred to work as ongoing conflict. When this propaganda is no longer believed, peace and harmony ensues. What we choose to focus on determines our life experiences. Confidence and clarity are possible amidst all the confusion. People doubt their own God self. Christianity requires personal crucifixion to work. Many experience life as birth, crucifixion, death, and reincarnation through denial and the conviction that there is past, present, and future. The ego knows it is preceded by something, that the present is an interpretation, and that something follows after it has passed away. This story is not easy to overcome. All kinds of interpretations are made by all kinds of people. Again, success is measured by how many people subscribe to and support the ideas of others. Institutions stand from the ideas people have stated that many feel are 'it' and the way existence is. Yet, no two people are the same, so no two people live and experience life identically. The ego is only interested in getting from externally, so that it feels its existence is justified and re-enforced by ideas that often have no relevance to the individual.

Interpretation is a very curious oxymoron. My interpretation will differ from anyone else's. Many allow the ego of another to dictate and determine what is real and true. What happens is that most miss the point of infinity as God's I Am- ness. This can be thought of as individuality versus collective consciousness. There is the universal and the specific we each live as our self and ego. Creation can be thought of as oneness, binary vibrancy, the fourfold, and then infinity. The numerology of this is 1, 2, 4, 8, 16, 32, 64, 128 etc. This is the law of doubling. What the creation seeks to do is increase the mass and magnitude of love/light- light/love. The flip side of this is how people negatively increase their power. They need people to deny their own love, light, reality, and truth, thereby giving their power away to someone or something else. People accomplish this by placing their faith in anything that is external.

Invading the Indigenous while the Rest of Us Watch

Externals require that we bow down to them in subjugation. Many false gods insist upon this type of behavior. Hierarchy and elitism are contrasted by equality and balance. The ideals composing the invader culture are hierarchy, elitism, superiority, chosen-ness, and good versus evil, leading to conquering, enslaving, and destroying through fear, judgment, and persecution. The ideals composing the indigenous way of being are equality, balance, relationship, purpose, and harmony, leading to peace, serenity, and tranquility through joy, love, and happiness. Both ways of being require discipline and development.

Within the indigenous culture is the integrity of the body and the connected integration it has with the environment. This is completely lacking with people living as part of the invader culture. Disease is the result of people living at odds with their humanness. Life contributes to life through the act of predation. The invader culture states that this is survival of the fittest. The fact is making a contribution is the only way "life according to species" works. This is something humanity does not understand now. The sacrificing of one's life for the betterment of humanity can be noble when it is not based upon denial. Ascension is the wiser way to go. Martyrdom is often done for misguided reasons. Allowing the death of the body shows a lack of love and wisdom on the part of the individual. People do not know any better, so death as an end is not healed. Most of what afflicts people usually remains unhealed. Anything unresolved will be carried over into the next life as karma. In one sense, the ego is what we are here to karmicly heal during our life.

Making a commitment is not easy. People observe both the invader and the indigenous as a way of being and living. Few consciously choose to adopt either as their way of life. Life evolves according to path and purpose. The path is going within; purpose is how this is shared with others. Knowing the self is part of why we are here. Serving others is also an aspect of our existence. Aspiring to ascend individually or collectively culminates the human drama. Most people go about their business oblivious to these larger opportunities. Many people are comfortably numb. Many only follow the dictates of some ideology. Many refuse to heal what is only meant to act as a catalyst so that one can evolve beyond what it is as an experience. When life is outgrown, it is time to move on. This is real evolution. Not the display of infinity shown through the incremental changes science considers evolution, which it is not. Evolution is how the physical evolves from something planetary into something eternal and ongoing as-is.

The indigenous way of life is based upon equality, balance, relationship, purpose, and harmony according to the intention of the creator. The bestower's role in this is bringing to life what was created as an ideal that evolves according to the environment within which the culture lives. For each indigenous culture, this will differ depending on what kind of environment each lives within. The spirituality of the indigenous is based upon life itself. There is a direct correspondence between the community of the indigenous and the environment within which it plays. This is the connected integration of the members and every life form composing the culture's planetary existence. Every invader culture has considered this barbaric and pagan. Peaceful cohabitation was the early way of every indigenous culture before the invader culture mindset infected the beliefs of original man.

Historically, invaders lived by warfare as social behavior, which the indigenous then adopted as rites of passage from adolescence to manhood. Taking the life of something as either animal or human is considered the rite of passage from child to adult in many cultures. But a stark contrast exists between invader cultures and indigenous people. Invader cultures are very complex, whereas indigenous people live very simply. The needs of the many are more important than the arrogance of the few. This also can be thought of as family equals the community, rather than the ego establishing itself as a false god that many worship as a graven image.

What are the qualities revered within the indigenous culture that establishes its entire sense of identity? The conflict we all face is between beliefs and truth. Many ideas are only forms of superstition based upon fear. Both cultures have them. People have

Invading the Indigenous while the Rest of Us Watch

the opportunity and responsibility of evolving consciously beyond ideologies of limitation. Oftentimes, one has to leave the community of birth to discover and own what is real and true as it involves and corresponds to one's life and existence. The introduction of new ideas into cultures steeped in fear and denial is next to impossible. This is why evolution is so slow or nonexistent for most people and most cultures. The idea or notion of changing something within a culture when there is reverence for dogma does not happen.

Humanity will discover very soon that life as this planet will evolve beyond the fictions lived by so many.

Humanity will return to living as designed. Those who are not harvested will become extinct. Humanness and biology will evolve and ascend as the connected integration it has always existed as, ideologically. The indigenous are the blueprint originally created long ago. Those living indigenously have remained true to their inherent way of life. The indigenous are how we were originally created to live, humanly. This can be thought of as living negatively as the invader, positively as the indigenous, or arbitrarily as the rest of us. Those indigenous people who adopted the invader culture way as their way have all

become extinct.

Wise teachers come to demonstrate one ideal: to stand as a living testimony to what is real and true humanly. Few understand the roles of the positive, the negative, or the arbitrary as one's way of life. This ensures the death experience personally, and in our day and age, our extinction. Again, the irony of this is that the Bible is composed of the three same points of view. The Old Testament is negative, the life of Jesus is positive, and Paul's theology was arbitrary. Each of us gets to choose what we feel, think, and act on, humanly.

The Intuit of Alaska and the Aboriginal of Australia still have the ability to move about over large areas of terrain. Most of the Native Americans of North America live on fixed reservations. This prevents them from living a life of adaptation to the environment. Movement is the change of evolution, which is the infinitude of experience. Instant replay is the marvel of television, not the progress of evolution as it changes into greater levels of self-expression. Ideals, as expressed, are always created and brought to life. Evolution is how the biological changes into what is eternal and ongoing. It is the body and spirit, as love and light, which evolves through ascension.

The will to be is love; the will to know is light. Consciousness is the awareness of these as self, existing as holographic structure giving one the perception of time and space, i.e., durated placement. This allows for individual development until it organizes into collective wisdom.

Indigenous people demonstrate our original design. Invader cultures live according to false doctrine. The rest of us live according to arbitrary ideas. These three ways of life all evolve side by side until the ending of false doctrine and arbitrariness in the year 2012. Humanity will return to living as it was created to exist, humanly. This will be a return to living indigenously. What ends, humanly, is the invader culture and everything it stands for, destroyed by the ideologies it supports and reveres. This is no different than the death experience for the average person. Beliefs are the basis for death when died for through conviction. Even when we know "the dead bury the dead; God is only of the living." Heaven is reserved only for those unwilling to live humanly as designed and brought to life. Those people who choose to live only as their ego.

I have always appreciated the simplicity and holisticness of most indigenous people. Their ways of community and environmental interaction always strike me as appropriate. Cultural diversity is the human factor of infinity-that and individuality. This culminates in synthesis of endeavor, where community emerges out of the personally conducive. I have always liked the idea of the Great Spirit of the Native Americans, their sense of connectedness to the land and animals, how everything in nature was treated with respect, reverence, and sacredness. This is missing from most of the rest of humanity. Much of what we see displayed humanly is

Invading the Indigenous while the Rest of Us Watch

negative and ugly forms of insanity revered as the way it is for the selfish, ignorant, and dying.

(When looking at or studying human being-ness, what is essential to this is what ascends. Evolution is what infinity does over time through space. What people do is ascend individually or collectively.)

The indigenous way of life is how we were created to exist as humanly. This shows us what connected integration is and how it works relationally and environmentally. What we observe, as contrast between both cultures, is simplicity and the ability to move, versus complexity and fixation. This is the cultural evolution of both ways of life observed from an arbitrary point of view.

The question we all need to ask is: Why did indigenous people live prior to the arrival of every invader culture historically? I offer that it was to show us how to live humanly on this planet. The arrival of Europeans to America provided the opportunity of adopting the indigenous way of living, rather than transplanting ideologies from Europe that did not work then or now. In this, people have missed the point entirely about why cultures exist, and what is accomplished through misguided ideologies that make every invader culture what it is.

The indigenous way of life adapts itself to its environment. The invader culture mindset is conquering nature and people. One striking difference between both ways of life is how much waste is generated, compared to how everything is utilized completely so that there is little or no waste at all. Living indigenously is living naturally, whereas living as an invader means living artificially, which requires replacing principles of integrity with arbitrary rules acting as law through a lack of love and light lived. This can be thought of as eradicating what is true with all kinds of ideas that are arbitrary and man-made. This is the contrast we now observe between science and technology and the simplicity of living indigenously. This is also what the ego has accomplished for most of humanity.

Douglas H. Melloy

The indigenous are the original design, living as the true image and likeness of God. Humanity will return to living this way very soon, quite possibly as early as mid December 2012. Very few people will make the transition due to a lack of understanding of what ends humanly and why. Only about 0.7 percent will survive out of seven billion people. People will not just suddenly disappear into thin air. Only those whose evolution matches what comes will remain to continue the evolution of human being-ness until it collectively ascends, around the year 3000.

Invading the Indigenous while the Rest of Us Watch

Indigenous Ideology

Very little was actually owned by the average indigenous person. Only what was needed was considered of importance, like food, clothing, and shelter. There were items of spiritual significance, like medicine bundles and handcrafted gifts having personal significance. Exchange was always done through bartering, which is much more evolved than financial exchange. Money only exists to establish class distinction and control through debt. The contrast between the two cultures is either "taking possession of" or "being in possession of." The ego lives according to the notion that it is here to get from God, planet, people, or some other divine agency. This determines what kind of humanity a person actually lives. The misguided live the folly of ownership, acquisition, and entitlement, granted through those in power. Within the framework of indigenous people, that which is the possession of one belongs to the entire clan or tribe. This was always the equal distribution of wealth to all members. This contrast is observed as the selfishness of one, versus the integrity of the collective. It is only the ego and its arrogance that feels that socialism is erroneous and evil.

The underlying ideology of the invader culture is survival of the fittest. Within the organism of the indigenous, the entire tribe is considered one ideal. In the early development of the indigenous, there was not gender disparity. Both sexes were considered equal and balanced. With the advancement of the invader culture, inequality and imbalance became the personal and social status of a group of people, established as a hierarchy of elitism convinced of its superiority and considered favored by God. Those living indigenously only recognized life and people as equalitarian, meaning that everything was equal to everything. There was no greater and lesser. Remember that, in a medium that is infinite, nothing has greater or lesser value than anything else. A grain of sand has as much value as an entire planet or universe. Only the foolish believe and act otherwise. The role of the ego is placing judgment on people, places, and things by giving value to ideals. This is the sophistication of the arrogance of those who believe they are superior to others.

There is that element within a clan or tribe where role-playing is determined by gender and accomplishment. After the infection of the invader culture, this was converted into the warrior mentality. Acts of aggression are contrary to our design. It is a learned form of behavior. Those who think humanness is innately evil or bad/selfish do not know much of anything about our design and its natural tendency towards kindness. This can be thought of as egoic individuality versus the Christ. The Christ is the collective consciousness of humanity living its original nature, which is love and light. Any group of people that lived peacefully and harmoniously demonstrated the Christ as that collective. The measure of a person is that contribution made to others without expectation of want for self- interested gain.

Reverence, sacredness, and respect are the basis for the cultural development of an indigenous people. Invaders lack these qualities entirely. Within the indigenous way of life, members contribute to the tribe or clan as a whole, as a single entity. Selfishness is considered inappropriate. Achievement only has relevance within the context of the collective and how it can assist it in its wholesomeness. Within the invader culture, the emphasis is on the ego and how godlike it becomes. The only aspect worshipped within the indigenous was the Great Spirit. This was replaced by the worshipping of false gods-within most cultures eventually. The pervasiveness of false doctrine now is worldwide. False doctrine is any idea or group of ideas, established as a systems theory within a tradition that people believe in for thousands of years that are not based upon intuition or personal experience. They are systems of ideology that are not based upon who we are.

The role of ceremony was essential to the indigenous way of life. This was a way of showing respect to life, one's ancestors, and the engagement within the tribe. The fact is, the indigenous are here to teach the rest of us how to live humanly and humanely. This requires knowing what it is to be human. The interesting quality about indigenous spirituality is that it is something very much alive and living. The spirit of any animal hunted was always respected after it was killed. There was always gratitude for its giving its life for the health and survival of the tribe. Contrasted against this is the religiosity of the invader culture and its emphasis on worshipping a god that is jealous, vengeful, and war-like-a god that allows his only begotten son to be crucified. The emphasis is on death, not life; on punishment, not on the innocence in being human.

Symbolic meaning is an important aspect of the indigenous ideology. Symbols give form to what usually remains esoteric and divine. Symbols can also be archetypes. These are underlying representations of human imagination, giving imagery to psychological interpretations about the unknown and mysterious nature of existence. Dreaming is considered a true state of our existence according to some indigenous cultures. They know that dreaming is the soul communicating to the ego. When the soul is known, dreaming is no longer needed or necessary. Dreaming ceases, as it is no longer useful to the consciousness of the individual.

There is a division between the two cultures that separates the inner and the outer. Realness and truth are within. Falsity and illusion are without. Within each culture, there are shortcomings from not taking enough into consideration about humanness and its role on this planet. People are given the opportunity to adopt from both cultures what is useful in evolving the species.

****

Evolution is the only aspect of relevance when considering humanness and what it becomes. What is considered are the elements or components that make our ideal what it is as an evolving human being-ness. Useful in answering this is addressing the ideas of God, universe, what created us, and what brought us to life. All four are involved. Each differs from the other. Compounding this are the truths of oneness and perfection.

The primary social traits of the indigenous are that of hunter/gatherers. Contrasting this is the acquiring nature of the invader. I call this the syndrome of the king and queen. Many aspire to become kings or queens of their domains. It is coexistence versus the building of an empire. Indigenous living requires coexistence with people and land. Living as an invader requires the subjugation of people and conquering the land. Both ways of life serve their purposes. People either seek to be their true natures, or they intend to build empires according to an ego seeking glorification and idol worship. Living indigenously requires equality, balance, and harmony amongst its members. Peacefulness is the way of those who truly live as designed. Lack of ownership is also what distinguishes the indigenous way of life. Energy is never owned. It only represents an ideal that is personal, relational, social, global, and finally, universal. These all coexist simultaneously.

Simplicity is positive. Complexity is negative. Anything goes when living arbitrarily. This is the format of the Bible, with the Old Testament, life of Jesus, and the theology of Paul. In a given moment, we are positive, negative, or arbitrary about our life and the lives of others. It is by design and is why there is free will, humanly. We choose what we get involved with and why. Usually we fail to get it about what is actually going on with organizations, our life, and evolution. We simply do not understand what service polarity entails as social evolution through class identification. The indigenous live their way even after being invaded and conquered by self-serving individuals who have socialized the unsuspecting into doing their bidding. Many fool others into following them under the guise that they are chosen by God to do so. This is only ego worship. This is referred to as idolization and graven imagery as those who are egotistical always end up dead and buried.

The actual conflict pursuant involves either living with nature according to one's biology, or the notion that nature must be conquered and controlled. Controlled manipulation is the way of the

Invading the Indigenous while the Rest of Us Watch

invader culture mindset. This is contrasted by creative manifestation. The created becomes what the self-serving control by 'divine right.' It is also the entire premise of the 'holy war.' The indigenous are how humans were created to exist on this planet through the love of Yahweh and the light of Id. This is our embodied spirituality. This is unified with willing ensoul-ment. The creative force is the will of God existing as the mind. The soul is conscious-awareness mated within the body. It is the only soul mate relationship one ever actually has, humanly. The confusion about this is denial that becomes projected objectification that is feared.

Fear is the great obstacle to personal and social evolution. The role it plays within the creation is that it allows love to exist in independent and differing ways that are unique. Fear and darkness allow love and light their individuality and unique ways of experience and expression. (The vision I was given when my heart chakra opened completely was love and light shaking hands with fear and darkness. I was also surprised by the size of this chakra. It completely filled the entire chest area, like a dinner plate.) Fear, in and of itself, does not exist. Fear as a face is the ego. Death is the ego getting even with itself! Unresolved fear is the death experience through taking what life is as our human being-ness. Fear takes the body with it when it goes, just as love takes the body with it when it ascends. Fear is that agency that breaks energy down, so that what is within it, God, can evolve into greater levels of self-expression.

Anyone who claims the body is left behind does not know what ascension is. Ascension is and means: rising above, to take with, and integrating into. What are risen above are lower states of consciousness. What is taken with one is hiser body as the love it is. What is integrated into is the larger reality of the universe, because what ascends is infinite and eternal as an ongoing-ness.

Individuality is always conflicted by collective consciousness. This is demonstrated by how much of the brain is active and dormant. The average person only uses 6 percent to 10 percent of hiser brain. The 90 to 94 percent that is dormant involves and pertains to the collective nature of the self. Lacking utilization of the entire brain ensures that the death experience will transpire. Everyone is responsible for ending hiser death experience. This is done through embracing and owning oneness coupled with the truth of perfection-not as absolutes. This can also be thought of as opening the heart and activating the brain by choosing to live what they are as aspects of our life.

The way of life lived centers around how people choose to exist humanly. This is done according to the negativity of the invader culture, the positivity of the indigenous culture, or the arbitrariness of the rest of us. Before the introduction of the invader culture mindset through the warlord god Jehovah, indigenous people lived peacefully and harmoniously. Eventually, the invader way of living infected the lifestyle of those who are our original design. Ending the invader culture mindset requires eliminating all the ideas and ideologies making it what it is. Specifically, fear, judgment, and persecution through war, greed, and class distinction based upon the figments of separation, survival, and selfishness. Often times what began as a positive activity was perverted into rituals of abuse, like cutting the heart out of people and chopping their heads off. The actual teaching was opening the heart to love, and activating the brain to light. The original teaching began in Egypt with the creating of the Great Pyramid by the entity know as RA. RA Material/Law of One.

The end times that are prophesied about only separate what is untenable from what is eternal and ongoing, which is what corresponds to the natures of both Yahweh our creator, and Id, our bestower; who brought us to life as the human being-ness we are. Many aspire to be false gods, like Jehovah. Many have only succeeded in the glorification of their egos as false idols and graven images. Fear acts like a barnacle. It attaches itself to ideologies to reinforce it and maintain it to the death. It is only fear as the ego that produces death. Our attachment to our ego ensures that each of us will die. What each of us gets to resolve is denial, fear, arrogance, and selfishness. This is the basis for the invader culture from the perspective of the individual. Hierarchy, elitism, superiority, chosen-ness, and good versus evil, coupled with conquering, enslaving, and

Invading the Indigenous while the Rest of Us Watch

destroying others compose the invader culture mindset. This is what ends humanly on this planet as the end times.

Humanity will return to living indigenously, as this is our original design as created by Yahweh and brought to life by Id 75,000 years ago. (Again, the time frame is according to the RA Material/Law of One. L/L Research. Carla Reuckert- McCarty channel.) This will happen when the invader cultures of this planet and all who support them become extinct, like the dinosaurs. Mary Summer Rain also posits the truth of our returning to living indigenously. There are also other sources, like the Hopi and the entities committed to our eventual collective ascension, which are simply souls committed to evolving beyond the limitations of the ego and its fear and arrogance.

This requires the understanding that the body and the earth are the same. Also, that it is the same spirit that gave us life, and that we are each other. That there is only one of us here, and each of us is that one, and that love is the physical and light is the spiritual within the infinitude of God existing as all that is. That greater and lesser are impossible within a medium that is infinite. That abundance is the contribution we make to each other. That everyone has as much value as anyone else, and we all live and stand on sacred, common ground. Also, that there is a connected integration with all of the various life forms that make biological life what it is here. These are the basis for the indigenous culture way of life. This is something most people have completely lost sight of now. Humanity returns to its natural way of being, knowing, and sharing very, very soon.

The contrast between the natural and the artificial is stunning to observe. Great city-states stand, with their millions of people. These create mass consciousness and everything unnatural to our experience and existence. There is a palpable denseness that envelops everyone living within the confines of that environment of steel, glass, cement, asphalt, and plastic. I suspect that every city/town/nation is a version or form of Sodom and Gomorrah. Low-density populations allow one to feel stillness, peace, and harmony wherever one is when mass consciousness is absent. Artificiality requires contrived fictions of concern, competition, confusion, and conflict. It is the invader culture way of existing. Always, there is a threat one has to protect and defend hiser self against one's own fear. The perpetrator always comes along to 'save' one from hiser imaginary plights of fear, felt as real, and one's dysfunctional imagination. This requires making something to fear, Satan, and then protecting one against what one has made as that.

How does an idea or ideal work as an ideology within the organism as a whole, either as the personal or the social? What is its compatibility and ongoing-ness? Answering these questions requires knowing what composes the existence of one's life, and then seeing how the truth of it works for everything involved within a stipulated reality. This is not as easy to do as so many claim it is when they are clueless, due to lacking the art of stillness and of relying on the intuition for insight and guidance. Life giving to life is the indigenous understanding of the hunter mindset. This is how life contributes to itself through predation. Everything contributes to everything for the sake of the common good of life itself. Making a contribution is the creation and how it works. This is called service polarity when the decision is consciously made to either empower the ego or contribute to others humbly and transparently.

Within the framework of cultural development, this is determined by the role of the composing members. Each has hiser responsibility within the group to contribute those talents inherent within. To effectively establish integration within the group, tribe, or clan, resolving issues is also necessary. This is where ethics, morality, and integrity apply. Every group has their own version of what these are and how they work for the group as a whole and the individual. Everyone decides on what kind of rituals he or she will perform within hiser life according to the traditions subscribed and adhered to personally and socially. Religion exists for two specific reasons one's fear of death and God. Tradition is made up of the rituals of conformity, demand, and human sacrifice for ideologies that are pure nonsense and make believe. Evolution requires leaving

Invading the Indigenous while the Rest of Us Watch

the ideas of the past, which are the experiences of those who have died, buried with them.

(This is not easy to do. The ego holds to the ideas of past, present, and future, for it knows it is preceded by something, it is presently an ideal, and existence continues after it is gone. The ego is bound by time and space. Its existence is based on giving specific-ness a face. This is a point of observation that allows specific- ness to see what composes the overall self.)

The observation of the invader/indigenous dynamic is fascinating to watch. Seeing the positive and negative at work is good therapy. The rest of humanity lives arbitrarily. This dynamic is further complicated by service polarity. Again, the adage is this: "The measure of a man or woman is that contribution he or she makes to his or her fellow man without expectation or want for self-interested gain." Many miss this point about human evolution. Choosing service polarity is a requirement if one hopes to evolve. Lacking this, evolution will not happen. Making a contribution is what the creation does for itself through ideation. Evolution is another name for change. Creativity evolves through growth. These are the changes made throughout one's life. Lacking personal evolution leads to the scenario of birth, crucifixion, death, and reincarnation.

The indigenous way of life is the connected integration of the tribe and environment. It is also communal cohabitation of the people composing the community. There is also the respect the members have for each other, and the sacredness of spirituality that allows life to exist and flourish. There is only one spirit, just as there is only one of us here, and only one people. To live this requires cooperation and getting along with differences in culture, gender, and personality. It is the whole that benefits, along with everyone. The indigenous live according to the efficiency of use, taking only what is needed in the moment. The environment is left intact rather than being altered for self-serving purposes. The emphasis within the indigenous is on food, clothing, shelter, the roles members perform, ancestor worship, ritual, artistry, spirituality, and their connectedness to the spirit of place as biological synthesis. This is completely lacking within the invader culture mindset, with its ways of conquering, enslaving, and destroying nature and peoples.

The earth changes coming are in direct proportion to the number of people supporting and contributing to the invader culture mindset. What returns is the garden state and humanity living life as it was created to exist, biologically and humanly. This means everything artificial will fade away, becoming extinct. The changes coming will demonstrate the un-viability and untenable-ness of the invader culture. Humanity will return to its indigenous intention according to our true design. Hatred and false doctrine will cease to be what predominates our lives. Humanity will return to living as being God, life, humanness as the Christ, serving others, oneness, healing, and wholeness that collectively ascends.

Invading the Indigenous while the Rest of Us Watch

Returning

Collective ascension requires the elimination of every ideology that is contrary to what it is as an ongoing realness. That which is contrary to collective ascension is race distinction, gender disparity, bias, nationalism, ego glorification, idol worship, the belief in opposites in conflict, ownership, competition, violence, disease, poverty, greed, division, arbitrariness, the notion of either-or, absoluteness, class distinction, survival of the fittest, disenfranchisement, and extremism. These prevent the possibility of collective ascension ever taking place. The irony is that collective ascension is positive human evolution. Individual ascension is more negative than positive. Individual representations are more negative than positive for anything existing within the universe. Individuality will only evolve so far within the creation. Again, according to The RA Material, individuality ceases to exist at the fourth octave of sixth density, as it is here that love and light are unified. This means that individuality only exists as an ideal up to the third octave of sixth density.

People are responsible for resolving individuality into understanding what collective consciousness is as the infinitude of the soul. Accomplishing this requires doing conscious out-of-body experiences. A common mistake people make is in thinking the mind and the ego are the same. They are not. The mind is God, and is represented as the heart. Becoming God-conscious is the Immaculate Conception and only takes place in the heart. This becomes the conversion experience, whereby one's life is converted into being God humanly. One becomes a God-man or woman. God-planet-universe, individualized and identified, is the life each person is, humanly. Few escape the fallacy of the ego and our over-identification with it. It is our false god. It is the premise on which all the gods we worship are based. The God that created the universe is never jealous and only loves Itself as what represents God infinitely. Everything within the universe is the image and likeness of God. We then choose to love God as this, fear God as this, or we are arbitrary about God existing as all that is. Our attitude about ourselves is what we feel about God, life, others, and creation. The mind is God, the spirit is oneness, and it brings to life what is created so that it can act as something independent and unique. The soul is the universal existing as something specific. The body is the image and likeness of the creator, Yahweh, and the bestower, Id, that brought what Yahweh created to life. The ego is the perspective our individualized uniqueness holds that considers itself an absolute.

The emphasis on controlled manipulation prevents humanity from evolving. Its focus is death, destruction, and disaster. Chaos and mayhem are the smokescreens for agenda. The agenda is enslavement and false godhood. It is the glorification of the ego into a demigod.

The art of living is how well people get along and what contribution is made within the culture without over-glorifying the ego. Within the indigenous culture, everyone is respected for who they are, and role-playing is honored. The entire tribe exists as one integrated whole or family. It is the collective state of the tribe that is understood and respected. Then limitation comes with other people. Cultures live mutually exclusive to one another. There is only the family of humanity existing as the Christ consciousness. Race is a format, as is gender. We evolve by moving beyond outer appearances, which are only the masks we wear as our ego. My humanity is the humanity of everyone, regardless of what is lived. This is where love comes in, as it accepts unconditionally the differences of itself as this creation and all that is. Light remains even-minded about itself as diversification. Acceptance, even-minded-ness, responsibility, contribution, and purpose are one's path to embody and share. The civilized and pagan must resolve their differences into a synthesized wholesomeness. Getting along and aiming at contribution are all

Invading the Indigenous while the Rest of Us Watch

that matters socially. Our unwillingness to do this shows our lack of personal and social evolution.

God, life, humanness, and service are keys to how well humanity evolves. Anyone who is lacking an experience of these as hiser life has work to do. These extend and expand from person to person until humanity as a whole represents these socially. These then ascend collectively as a single state of being. They can be thought of as will, love, light, and consciousness, or sun, earth, moon, and universe. The representation of this is all we accomplish humanly as our identity and individuality. It is our belief in limitation that hinders our ability to be God and know the universe as our human being-ness, coupled with the divinity of love and the deity of light.

Our returning to living as designed is eminent. The indigenous show us how and what that is. It is a return to living simply and healthily, where negativity is minimized and the earth is treated with dignity. Each of us has to decide what is important and to work at becoming the humanity of that, according to our creation. This is being love and knowing light as our life, in conjunction with the will of God and the soul's consciousness of itself as human and all else. Not easy to do, as we are convinced we are anything but God and universe. The invader culture has convinced us we are all destined to die after living a life of fear, guilt, arrogance, and denial. Heaven only exists for those who are too afraid to live love/light as hiser life. People choose and commit themselves to those social orders they participate with, humanly. This is also required with the two cultures that are evolving on this planet.

Douglas H. Melloy

Part III:

The rest of us

Invading the Indigenous while the Rest of Us Watch

Arbitrariness:

Beliefs; Catalysts; Experience; Opposites in Harmony; Illusion; Free Will

Arbitrariness is the obstacle most of humanity fails to address and heal. People live negatively, positively, or arbitrarily. In a given moment, we choose how we feel as the positive, negative, or arbitrary. Again, the Bible can be thought of in this way. It is like we live as the Old Testament, the life of Jesus, or the arbitrariness of Paul.

Souls come to this planet to experience life humanly and to add to the evolution of our species. It is left to each of us to decide what is so about something, like God and life on this planet. We are left alone so we can make up our minds about what is. Influences abound, like our parents, family, institutions, interests, karma, and social involvements. We have our ideas, and ideas come to us. Life divides between the external world of the ego and what is inherent as the self. People gravitate to what agrees with them. This gives reinforcement to what is believed. People look for protection from their fear. Some want to be 'saved' from hiser self. The wilderness is foreboding. We stand, measuring ourselves against others to see how our life measures up. Our attention is continuously pulled to outer circumstances that we do not understand. There is the veil of forgetfulness, so the soul does not know itself. There is the veil of confusion, so the ego does not understand. There is the veil of access, so God remains foreign to Itself as Its humanness. Life is, and we do not get it.

Contrariness is the way of existence for those whose life is affected by unresolved catalysts. We have many to resolve. Issues of hindrance bog us down through our resistance to them. 'Talents remain ignored and dormant. Making sense of life and our existence seems impossible to do. We try to find meaning and purpose within the chaos. Always, we are looking for the greener grass that changes when we get close to it. Traditions tell us this is it, but infinity informs us there is always something else and something more. Someone 'discovers' the obvious, and we decide that hiser view is it-the one for us to believe to the grave. Our life. differs from any other, yet we conform it to the dictates of those who we feel 'know,' so we remain lost in our own denial and fear. The ego knows that it is nothing, so externals as the obvious is only what it relies on for reality and truth.

Where are the love, forgiveness, and doing unto others within the crucifixion? Odd that this is the symbol worshipped by Christians. It is a symbol of guilt, cruelty, torture, suffering, and death. It is what Christians aspire to humanly, not innocence, humility, kindness, wonderful-ism, and ascension. Something only has the value it is given as an importance to the individual. Reality is self-defined as a personal truth that remains ignored, denied, and feared. Belief confines. It limits one's ability to be, know, share, and ascend. Infinity is variable and a variety of that which remains constant. It is also the differentiation of God into the infinite, so that God can experience I Am-ness infinitely. We then decide what to feel, think, and act upon regarding and involving God as what surrounds us. This is the planet itself, as well as everything existing on the surface as biological life and our humanity.

Arbitrarily, we forge ahead to our doom, unaware that reality and truth are our life. Nothing makes any sense, yet we hold to figments of our imagination that are only fictions proven to us. Our convictions are so steadfast that we miss the point of reality completely. Intuition is discounted or denied. The evidence relied upon is illusion. Addictions, distractions, and dysfunctions remain unhealed. Anything goes. So caught up with the external are we that the internal remains only a place of indigestion and heartburn. Lack, need, want, and wound remain unchanged, personally and socially. Then, we wonder why nothing works very well for us, humanly. Individuality, as identity, fools us into ignoring and denying the nature of the self and how it evolves personally, relationally, socially, globally, and universally. It is not our fault. We do not know any better, so nothing changes, and now it is too late!

Again, "Nothing is inappropriate given one's measure of the world," God tells Neale Donald Walsch in Conversations With God. Nothing is acceptable to us, yet everything is acceptable to God through love, as this is all and only what love does with everything and everyone. Fear, judgment, and persecution are the ways of man after its involvement with the warlord god Jehovah around 9,000 BC. Even after Jesus taught love, forgiveness, and doing unto others to resolve these, people still live them as their psychology. Jesus was the messiah for the Jewish people two thousand years ago. Their failure to recognize and realize this may now doom them as a people, just as today's Christian fails to realize that the second coming of Jesus actually took place right after his resurrection, and now is A Course In Miracles, published in 1975 by Foundation For Inner Peace.

If humanity lived love creatively, laws would not be necessary. Everything would take care of itself. Love and wisdom are the arts of appropriateness. It is like conflict exists between appropriateness and arbitrariness. Who aspires to wisdom, artistry, and kindness? Who desires to know the truth? Who knows what beauty is? Who amongst us is truly good? The irony is that everything is within us. Everything. It is just as easy to live positively and generously as it is any other way. Who grieves for humanity and this planet? Where is the passion for assisting others? Who is willing to sacrifice hiser life for the greater good? (Beauty is the observation of love and light reflected back to one, so that he or she will recognize hiser own.)

Douglas H. Melloy

(The third chakra is the Christ consciousness, humanly. The fourth chakra is content of character that is shared purposefully. The fifth chakra is the truth spoken when one knows what it is, humanly.) Each of us is responsible for hiser evolution-the development of consciousness through resolving issues and developing talents, coupled with embracing and owning those qualities, making our life honorable and authentic. This requires a working knowledge of what purpose negativity serves our life through catalysts. Asking what purpose a given experience serves one's life is wise. Another wisdom is owning up to what one contributes to hiser life through experiences. Life meets us where we stand as what we feel and think. This equals experience. When something takes place that is negative, we can ask ourselves what purpose does this experience serve my life? Then, wait for the answer to come. Not easy to do when faced with severe pain, fear, or animosity. It is never wise to accuse Satan for our negative experiences. Satan is the name we give to our fear when it is denied and then projected into an objectification that is then feared. The same can also be stated about God and good experiences. This is the role the ego plays for us as us. It is the false ideal of self that we have determined is our reality and truth.

Effective creativity requires a working knowledge of the will of God as our mind. This is used to create our experiences according to the blueprint of our soul. Life is not about getting whatever we want. It is all about effective creativity that has sustainability to it. This means understanding how energy works negatively, positively, and as something that is neutral. There is also self-reliance, or codependency. Understanding is compounded by the art of going it alone to embrace and own greater truths as the realness of being. People refuse to do so-so much of reality and truth remain nonexistent to one's point of view. The master-less path is the only valid one through meditation, pondering, and accepting responsibility for one's experiences. Over reliance upon externals, no matter how wise and enlightened, hinders one's path and purpose.

Uniqueness is infinity as a created and manifested ideal giving God Its I Am- ness. Individuality, as an identity, gives God Its

Invading the Indigenous while the Rest of Us Watch

sense of being. Everything in existence has an identity to represent what it is within the creation. The physical is love individuated and identified as the body. The spiritual is light individuated and identified, and what brings to life what is created. We see these as what is beautiful to us. Actually, all we are seeing is our love and light reflected back to us, so that we know these as our embodied spirituality, which is beautiful. The oneness of God is a state that is all encompassing existing as our mind. It is uniform and constant, never changing. It surrounds the universe and is centered within everything existent within the universe. Every sun/star is the original state of God individualized and identified. Centered within the heart is the same state of God waiting for us to bring it to life, converting our life to God. This is the Immaculate Conception and the conversion experience of human being into God being.

Life lived humanly is our make believe, as we believe whatever we want to, and it is always arbitrary. That is the way of most of humanity. It is the role of Paul in the Bible. Heaven and hell are fictions of the mind. The fears and guilt of people are played upon to keep the faithful enslaved and committed to an ideology that is false doctrine when it comes to God, life, humanness, and service. That is the role religion plays for the unenlightened and un-evolved. A given idea only has relevance to an individual for whatever reason he or she gives it. The flip side of belief is agreement. Experience is the only measure by which an idea has any value, meaning, or significance. Belief blinds one to an idea that has no relevance to the believer. Lacking experience, ideas are meaningless and irrelevant. Placing faith in the life of another, especially when he or she lived long ago, is pointless and ill advised. Truth, after it is realized, becomes pointless through the role evolution plays. One's life evolves beyond what it was in the moment. Once past, truth becomes an illusion. It is only our attachment to it that keeps it a fiction of the ego. A useful exercise is how easily we can let go of an idea so that greater truths through experience will come to us. This is the role evolution play, as it allows us to evolve beyond any truth realized as the past.

Douglas H. Melloy

A person's life is strictly hiser own. No two people are the same and no two people walk the same path, so why do so many people have the same faith? It is impossible for someone to become enlightened in the identical way as another. We are not Buddha, or Jesus, or any other wise soul from the past. The reality and truth we each personify differ according to our love and light lived. This is by design. Differentiation is the universe and God's intention. It is what we are here to accept and be even-minded about. Then, it becomes easy to love others. Reactive- ness will continue as long as we resist healing what we react to as our life. Again, that is why we are told, "What you resist, persists."

A good question to ask yourself is this: What is the agenda behind this information? Ask that with any body of knowledge with which you choose to involve yourself. The answers will come to you when you are ready to understand and accept them. Be prepared for what comes to you. Often, what does come invalidates our beliefs and that within which our faith is placed. Many are unwilling to allow for greater truth to come as one's life. This is the blind leading and following the blind. The blind are oblivious to what is real, true, and ongoing.

There is the perfection of how each person lives hiser life. It is a truly beautiful thing, seeing people live as they do-wonderful, in fact. Everyone is entitled to live exactly how he or she does. Personal nuances make humanness awesome and interesting. It is the nature of uniqueness to be different. It is also what infinity is. Variety is the spice of life. It also allows love to love itself as what it is not. Meaning that, anything that differs from us gives love the opportunity to love, because everything is an aspect of love and light made flesh and physical. This is missed by many due to holding onto the ego and its biasing of fear. This is healed when love is chosen. When observing something or someone, see that as the perfection it is in the moment. Also seek to be at one with it as an extension and expansion of your life. This is oneness and perfection owned, lived, and shared.

Invading the Indigenous while the Rest of Us Watch

Everything that surrounds us environmentally is the arbitrary. The heart is positive, the torso neutral, while the head is negative. When facing anything, know it is arbitrary. It is an outward projection of your inner being. It is only mirroring back to you who you are as that. Then, we choose what to feel about ourselves, as with everyone and everything. The art of being and living is how quickly we can move from what is negative into what is positive as our life. How quickly we can move from pain into joy, from fear into love, or from darkness into light is self-mastery. This requires knowing how to do it and, also, how binary vibrancy works. Doing a positive/negative meditation is very useful. Breathe in a positive quality, and exhale its opposite. Do this with as many terms as possible. Feel what they are, so you will know when you are feeling them. Then, when something negative presents itself to you, simply let it go and choose to be its positive twin. Every negative paths us to what is positive acting as catalysts for us to evolve beyond.

Many are resistant to doing this. They deny the contrast that is needed so that what is can be a living realness. Lacking an opposite, what is will never be known, humanly or otherwise. Our confusion comes from the belief of opposites in conflict, rather than opposites in harmony through inverse reversal existing as binary vibrancy that we experience as our heartbeat, breathing, waking and sleeping, and incarnation and ascension. Feeling is the path to God. Thinking is the path to the universe. When seeking, it is only done by going within. Those who seek by traveling afar for the wisdom of another will never find what they are seeking for, for it does not exist within another. "Seek for where I Am," we are advised, "Then you will find Me." Out there is an illusion, mirroring back to us our sense of identity. What we identify is God, universe, love, light, and everything we feel and think. These make our life what it is, humanly.

Douglas H. Melloy

God

What we role-play is energy as human. Some pretend to be negative, some arbitrary, and some positive. Life is anything we make it, according to energy. Energy conforms itself to our emotions and thoughts. Some are positive. Some are negative. Most are arbitrary. This is by design. It is the nature of free will, as it is this that allows us to live any way we choose to. The notion that we are supposed to live or be a certain way is pure nonsense! The idea of God only makes sense when it pertains to everything and everyone. God as an absolute, or an it is erroneous. God, originally, was a unifying idea. It still is. To know and understand this requires a working knowledge of God as an originating state and as a diversified state.

Currently, there are approximately ten thousand gods worshiped by people. None that are worshipped now correspond to our creator and bestower. "The one true God" is only understood through the experiences of all encompassing-ness and infinity. All encompassing-ness precedes the universe and now surrounds it. Infinity is the diversification of God into identity and individuality. What we identify are all the qualities we experience. What we individualize is God as mind, body, spirit, and soul. This gives us the opportunity to embrace God as God, and our life as our issues and talents, and all the catalysts that assist our evolution specifically and cosmically. Any idea about God requires the human element in order to have any relevance. This is also true of any idea. Lacking the human, the idea is nonsense. My mind is to God what my soul is to the universe, just as my love is to the physical what my spirit is to light. These are unified, connected, and integrated as my life, making me the humanness of them as one being. We are the unified field theory. We are the oneness of God, planet, and universe that lives path as purpose through being and knowing, that ascends.

Invading the Indigenous while the Rest of Us Watch

The art of arbitrariness confuses being with all sorts of ideas that misinforms us to the grave. God is currently in a state of rest. The active agency of God is the will. God's will extends and expands into love, then light. These become conscious. Consciousness is the awareness of itself as something specific and universal. Specificness allows its awareness to become more comprehensive. This is consciousness as a focus becoming aware of God and universe as the self, coupled with the ego.

This is who we are, humanly. The ego is our biological face that corresponds to our humanness according to this planet and our biological parents. The ego is the face of specific-ness and fear.

We are entitled to live any way desired. This is the art of free will. Humanness is all about experience and expression as the image and likeness of God. Everything in existence within the universe is an expression of God as an I Am-ness. These identify God individually and collectively. There is the existence of love, the identity of love, and the relationships that love has with differing versions of itself that we observe as infinity. Infinity is the diversification of God into all that is that we observe as our life, others, the biology of this planet, the planet itself, and the universe. These are all aspects of God. We then are positive, negative, or arbitrary about God's representations of Itself as everything observed. The path as purpose is whether we engage the creation in a destructive or creative manner. This is ignored by our involved insistence with small-minded pursuits of the ego.

Information is a curious thing in what it imparts to us. Some of it is relevant. Some of it is interesting and insightful. Most of it is false doctrine leading us astray, according to the agenda of the source. Few rely on their intuition. What is humanity evolving? There is an endless array of psychologies presenting their points of view. We agree, disagree, ignore, debate, contradict, or argue with them. Many are blinded by conviction and addicted to their ego. Entire systems theories stand as traditions that change very little over time. The intellect thrives on Da Vinci coding information into believable ideologies that many follow. Making sense of it all is ponderous and foreboding. The physical has one advantage over the spiritual. It allows for much quicker development and evolution when one is paying attention to hiser life. It is impossible to add to or take away from one's physical-ness and one's spirituality. Spirituality is oneness and activated uniqueness that seemingly exists independent of all else. The ego is convinced it is separated from all else, and that everything else is distanced from it. This is why the ego believes in time and space.

Life means love is forever evolving itself into greater levels of enlightened expressions of experience. These allow one to know what is so about life according to how one focuses upon it. Personal interests also give insight into what it is to be human on a planet. It is like we are getting our feet wet humanly. Trial and error is the way it is for all of us. We learn by example and experience. Many make the mistake of trying to follow in another's footsteps, or they seek to become just like whom they follow. Being true to one's own nature is not easy. Conformity is the expectation and demand from others. Family and peers pressure us to be their expectation. Many follow suit just so others will approve of their life as the choices they have made.

Meaning is self-determined; so are value, function, and purpose. The decisions we make about something are strictly our own. Our motivations are curious. Habitually, we ritualize our life in the hopes we are appeasing our sense of insecurity. Rituals are performed to keep our fear from demonizing us. Poor choices of the past continually haunt us. A friend of mine asked me if her violating one of the Ten Commandments dooms her to hell? My response was, why would God create a place that violated the realities of love, forgiveness, and doing unto others? Rules and laws are only necessary when fear is lived, rather than love. If God is love, then only love is created as what exists as the universe and our life. When love is lived and shared, it is only this we evolve into at greater levels of being and knowing. From the perspective of fear, love is felt as a very intense heat. Hell is the term fear uses to define and describe its relationship to love. The realness of love is unbearable

Invading the Indigenous while the Rest of Us Watch

to fear, so it is judged and persecuted. Fear and darkness allow love and light individualized identity. God's will creates love, will/love create light, will/love/light then become conscious, according to our design.

The universe is the creation of infinity as a contrast to God's all encompassing- ness, so that God can experience I Am-ness. We are God's humanness. We are the image and likeness of God making us God's I Am-ness, humanly. People differ due to the nature of infinity. This is true of all life forms, like grains of sand, snowflakes, blades of grass, or leaves of trees. It is our individuality and karma that determine what kind of involvement we will have with the environment and others. How one reconciles hiser specific-ness and the corresponding universe is part of the work one does consciously. It is not so much work, but rather applied intention to be and know what is real and true from one's perspective. This can be daunting to understand well enough to share with others.

The idea of absoluteness is also a great stumbling block for people. The ego only deals with single ideas considered absolute to its specific-ness. The ego also only relates to the concept of it through beliefs according to what one feels and thinks is hiser life, humanly. These are the measures by which one's entire life is lived.

Curiously, many people think only in terms of higher consciousness, rather than of collective insight and understanding, Individuality is a collective state unified into the oneness of the self/ego gestalt, which gives identity to those feelings and thoughts giving one hiser entire sense of being and knowing. Again, it is left to each of us to decide what is so about everything, including God and universe. Difficult to do when there are so many differing ideas about God as life lived as a human being. The self/ego gestalt exists because of Yahweh and Id and our biological parents. All four states of being are unified into our sense of identity. These four states make us the unified field theory.

****

Douglas H. Melloy

What we feel and think is left up to us. This is arbitrariness. It is up to each of us to decide for ourselves what is so with anything. But again, we do something curious; we seek agreement from others and are intolerant with anyone whose ideas and way of life differs from our own. The irony of this is that it is impossible for any two people to live the same life. Infinity does not do instant replay. So, why do so many aspire to be like Buddha, Jesus, Mohammed, or some other individual, past or present? Our life is the humanness of God and universe according to this planet. Anything that exists is inherent within us. If it is not within, it does not exist. The path is embracing and owning what is, thereby making our life the existence of as our being-ness. This requires meditation and honesty to be, know, share, and ascend. It also means letting go of the ego as our only sense of identity.

The path is going within to become conscious of what is inherent. Purpose is how this is shared with others without martyrdom or personal sacrifice. Allowing oneself to be killed is not how existence is well served. The life we live is as important as anything else. God's I Am-ness humanly is identified through each one of us. The entire universe is God's Identity represented as infinity. This is the diversification of God into all that is that we are consciously aware of personally as our biology on this planet. This allows us to recognize that love is expressed in an infinite number of ways within a given species, and divergently. Free will allows each of us to choose how we will live and why we live the way that we do. It is completely arbitrary due to our uniqueness and the blueprinting of the soul. Individuality evolves into collective agreement that ascends as one unified being. ness that is eternal.

Time and space exist because will exists independent of love, which is independent of light, which is independent of consciousness. These four states of being compose our life as the heart, torso, head, and awareness. Time is the duration of; space is the placement of, while awareness is how consciousness perceives itself as a created medium of intention. Time also means segmented documentation of movement, moment by moment, according to second, minute,

Invading the Indigenous while the Rest of Us Watch

hour, day, week, month, year, century, and millennia. Time and space do not exist within holographic structure and how it moves, evolves, and grows. We are the oneness of will, love, light, and consciousness, existing as the self-sustaining, self- regenerative, and self-perpetuating within what is instantaneous, spontaneous, and simultaneous now here being. The ego is convinced otherwise.

People live arbitrarily until they choose to polarize into the paths of negative or positive service. Only these are what evolve consciousness. Those who are familiar with the idea of the harvesting of souls usually do not know that it only involves those who have chosen service polarity. Those who serve positively are harvested as the wheat of humanity, to begin the evolution of humanness until it collectively ascends as the unification of independence into harmonious cooperation. Those who are negatively polarized are harvested by being removed and transplanted to that place that matches their service polarity. Those not harvested repeat third density on another planet. As stated earlier, the idea of the ending of the world pertains to and involves those who are not harvested. They will think this planet has been destroyed as there is no more coming back to earth through the process of birth and reincarnation. Death of the body and incarnation of the soul are identical. The body dies to its planetary nature and state. The soul dies to its universality. These are only altered states of consciousness, allowing awareness to be what it is, as it is, arbitrarily. The soul actually 'forgets' who it is and where it comes from.

Arbitrariness means anyone is entitled to live any way he or she chooses. It is why free will exists, as it allows us the freedom to be who we are according to our blueprint and our ego. Free will is also essential in choosing service polarity. Choice is also required when facing issues and deciding what the moment is and means. We continuously move into and out of experiences. The ability to choose wisely requires development and discipline. Uniqueness requires personal choice. This is utilizing God's will to create and manifest a life that is interesting, insightful, enjoyable, contributory, and evolving, as well as one that is very grounded. The physical is every bit as much the path as anything else. We demonstrate mindful purposefulness in the context of embodied spirituality that is consciously aware of itself as an ensoul-ment that humbly and transparently assists others. This is how we are created to live, share, and evolve.

Gratitude and appreciation go a long way in allowing people to live as they choose to. Those who think that God is jealous of someone, or takes offense, or that something is an abomination worship a false god. Negative attitudes attributed to God remake that into a falsity. Christians have done this with the warlord god Jehovah and with Jesus, "the son of man."True it is that Jesus taught positive ideals, but people have remade him into someone he was not. The consequences of following false idols only lead to the grave and to an afterlife that is also a figment of one's imagination. Humanity is warned about worshipping false idols and graven images, but the warning is discounted and ignored. The Old Testament teaches fearing God, whereas the New Testament teaches loving God and one another. Dying fear leads to the grave. Living love becomes what ascends. Heaven is the reward promised to those who accept that death is the inevitable. And almost every human being has died fear rather than lived love as the life he or she is..

Invading the Indigenous while the Rest of Us Watch

What the Rest of Us Just Don't 'Get'

The laws man has implemented over the centuries are just as arbitrary as those composing the rituals of religion. They go hand in hand. Fear and judgment stipulate, "Thou shalt not!" Free will makes "Thou shalt not", impossible. This is also true with the idea of 'sin. This ultimately applies to everyone. Humanness is the abomination of which the warlord god Jehovah is jealous, for this is not of His making. Hatred is what the warlord god Jehovah feels towards all and any things involving and pertaining to human being-ness. Death, disaster, and destruction are the makings of this false god, worshipped by two billion people. The question is why? It is Biblical, the "Word of God", we are told. The best the Christian can do is die and go to heaven to avoid going to hell. The faithful are rewarded, while those who do not follow are punished for eternity. Does any of that make any sense? The answer is no. Christian faith is the faith of avoidance, not the faith of the evidence of things not seen. Faith is knowing that God's will can be applied in creating those experiences one desires to embrace.

Living love renders religion unnecessary, as it is the ego's fear that makes religion an ideology of ritual and worship to appease the ego. Ritual is the reenactment of fear. No two people are the same, so why do five and a half billion people practice the four major religions of Hinduism, Buddhism, Christianity, and Islam? Secondary religions gobble up another billion people. Very few live according to infinity, with its making expressions unique and independent. Humanly, this requires living the being-ness of what is real and true, unlike any other. Love, when lived, means people will get along and be kind to one another. Differences between people will be loved rather than feared, honored rather than judged, contributed to rather than persecuted.

Douglas H. Melloy

Arbitrariness means we will live any way we choose to do, regardless of whether it corresponds to or involves what is real, true, and conducive to our human being-ness and the life on this planet. Eventually, arbitrariness gives way to our choosing negative or positive service polarity. This is accomplished through choosing either love or fear as the way it is. This is acted out humanly as either the ways of peace, drama, or war. The ways of the misguided do not realize that everything in life is a choice in being and knowing that is shared with others. What is believed determines how we engage and relate to others. Our attitudes about others only show how loving fearing we are about ourselves. This is also demonstrated by the disparities between the sexes and races of people. In a truly loving world, death, disease, and disharmony would not exist. The world we see today shows us all just how unloving we actually are. This is due to arbitrariness, denial, and arrogance. It is also due to the nature of the ego, which is arbitrariness lived.

The values we give to things are arbitrary in their measure. Why is gold given a value lusted after by so many? It is only a physical representation of peace embedded in the surface of the planet. That is why the Native Americans left it in the ground. The same goes with anything to which we give a value. Usually, what we value sets us apart from others. People hold to the repulsive nature of fear, rather than to the endearing quality of love. Pain convinces us we have separated from source. Fear tricks us into thinking we have been rejected by God. Darkness leads us to believe we are isolated and alone. Negativity is antagonistic. Guilt lets us know our karma is not resolved. Denial is the ego thinking it is an entity unto itself. The ego also feels it is a god. Many a false prophet cater to the whims of the ego. Many angelic beings take advantage of the unsuspecting as the source relied on for information that only leads people astray and enslaves those who allow deception to be their truth. The ego's fear is why God does not exist, or is only a false ideal. The ego is the graven image we idolize and worship.

Many do not realize the role negativity plays on earth as the invader culture mindset. Also, solitary nonphysical entities are more

Invading the Indigenous while the Rest of Us Watch

negative than positive. The information of solitary sources pales in comparison to collective sources that are channeled. This goes for any source sharing information. It is only the ego that is drawn to sources mirroring it. People ignore the truth of "As above, so below." Up there is no different than down here, as they are the same place and state of existence. People naively assume that life down here on earth differs completely than life up in heaven. Not so. People do not realize why they have an interest in things spiritual. Lacking an interest in something makes it impossible to expand one's awareness through experience to know what is so about it personally-especially when it comes to the mind, body, spirit, and soul. What is the individual identity of the mind, body, spirit, and soul? It is left to each of us to answer this question.

What is my life as God, planet, universe, divinity, deity, self, ego, for being human at this time? This is a very big question, taking some people many, many, many lifetimes to answer. People only think in terms of their ego. The ego is the body thinking of itself as something unique, special, other than, and at odds with all else. The ego is the mask that the body conceives of itself as, humanly. The irony of this is the body is the holograph of the mind. The ego is the effect of the body. Then, people do something very curious: they think in terms of their ego as if it were their identity, which it is not. Some make their ego a false god. There are those who ask people to follow them to the grave under the premise they will be rewarded in heaven for doing so. Only the 'living dead' die and go to heaven.

We cannot help ourselves. It is the way of the arbitrary and the negative. It is the path of those who only think in terms of ego and individualism. The law of attraction draws to us who we are, according to what is felt to be so about life, which is reinforced through experience and others, physically and spiritually. There is always a direct correspondence between what we feel we are humanly and the people and spirits we attract to us. Many an unsuspecting person give voice to negative sources, rather than positive. Many misinterpret what present themselves to those steeped in self-absorption. This can be thought of as individuality versus the Christ. Christ consciousness is the third chakra. It is also the collective consciousness of humanity when people, en masse, are being love and knowing light shared through service.

    The path is knowing the self and resolving the ego. Purpose is how this is shared, through contribution to others. Human evolution culminates in collective ascension. To accomplish this requires understanding how energy works as the positive and negative, according to what is arbitrary. Essential to effective service is humility and transparency. Anyone with an agenda only serves themselves through manipulation and contrived insistence. Those who play on the fears of people only do so to ensure continued involvement in order to empower themselves and glorify their ego. The ego of the self-serving becomes a false god worshipped as a graven image. What are lacking in one's awareness are discipline, discernment, and dedication to what is real and true as it pertains to human being-ness. This requires evolving beyond arbitrariness. A good place to start is questioning everything and everyone. The nature of who we are divides between what we are in possession of, and what we feel we need to get from others. These are the roles of the self and the ego. The ego only seeks to get from others any way it can. It will lie just to see what it gets from that. The ego lives the fiction of lusting after what others have acquired. Its motto is: "I am only here to get what you have, and I will do whatever it takes to accomplish this."

    One man's truth is another man's fiction. One person's experience is another person's illusion. What some people like, others dislike. Reality is self-defined as a personal truth. There is no getting away from this fact. Uniqueness ensures differences between people and individuals who identify what is, according to their makeup and inclination. The ego then tries to make this an absolute as an ideology or systems theory that others believe in as 'it.' The only idea that works when it comes to external information is to know that it is propaganda meant to see what you'll believe. Many believe ideas that are only that and nothing more. Truth is like a piece of a puzzle, according to the individual. Truth corresponds

Invading the Indigenous while the Rest of Us Watch

to individuality that is identified. Truth defines reality according to its designed intention. In our case, it is our humanness, which is what is evolving until it ascends, either individually or collectively. Individual ascension is more negative than positive always. Collective ascension is always positive. The specific does not have greater relevance or importance than the collective nature of existence or the self, which is the universal aspect of being. This becomes the Christ when people consciously choose to live love and light as their life through serving others. To do so effectively requires resolving the ego and its fear.

What gets in the way of this is self-importance and overemphasis upon the ego and on what one identifies as hiser life. Having an attitude or opinion about others is ridiculous because the only life we know is our own, and everyone is entitled to hiser experience. The ideas I entertain regarding and involving others is only about myself. People mirror back to us what we feel and think is our life as those. Love is always and only accepting of others. Light is always and only even-minded about what is 'out there,' reflecting back to us as our life as that. What are reflected back to us are both the personal and the social. This is reminiscent of the Seth book The Individual and the Nature of Mass Events. Mass consciousness has its effects upon those who live within its umbrella. Low-density populations are more conducive to personal development than high-density populations. The exception to this is when people gather together for an ideal that is based on love and light as the life each lives and contributes to others.

****

People do not do a very good job of understanding the mechanics of energy within the matrix of humanness. Energy is positive, negative, and neutral. As the body, energy is the positive heart, neutral torso, and negative head. Consciousness is the awareness of energy as it exists. Coupled with energy is arbitrariness. From the perspective of the ego, we are arbitrary in our way of living and knowing. The ego is awareness as consciousness that is specific and arbitrary. The ego is proof, humanly, that infinity exists. The ego is our arbitrary nature. According to it, nothing else exists. The ego is the specific-ness of our life as that which we feel, sense, think, and envision our life to be the experience and expression of. This will involve all our experiences. Experience is "the reality of" and "the truth about" as it pertains to our expression of life. For some, this is negative. For others, it is positive. For most, life is arbitrary.

The positive and negative unify into a neutral state that then evolves into service polarity. Again, only these two states of contribution are what evolve humanly. Service polarity is the wheat referred to in the Bible. The chaff pertains to everyone who refuses to polarize into either positive or negative service. This is tricky to understand, as there are two aspects to it. Those who are negatively polarized also are harvested. Negative polarization requires self-absorption, while those involved do not actually know what is going on with the ideology and its agenda.

Those who are not harvested repeat third density. Making a contribution is the only role of importance humanly. Our life is measured by the contributions we make to others selflessly. This is our time of harvest. Only those who serve others will be harvested to evolve our species until it collectively ascends. Everyone else will be removed. People who think their beliefs of faith save them or protect them are foolishly misguided. It is the content of our character and the contributions we make that determine our personal and social evolution. It is defined by what our life is based upon, humanly. For some, it is fear and darkness playing the roles of controlling manipulator. For others, it is love and light creating and manifesting a reality that is true and conducive, as well as ongoing.

Fear allows love to exist independently. Darkness allows light individuality. If fear and darkness are removed, the entire creation ceases to exist. Time and space exist because love and light are individualized and independent states of being and knowing. This allows God the experience of I Am-ness. Time and space are the duration of separation between what is perceived of as identified

Invading the Indigenous while the Rest of Us Watch

individuality, called the ego. Again, the ego gives us the sense we are different from all else and distanced from all else. It is our make believe. It is the role infinity plays for God. This seeks for one ideal-unification of Itself back into the oneness that it is. This is accomplished through collective ascension. Collective ascension is the unification of divergent states of being into the oneness of connected integration that exists as the infinite and eternal. This state will ascend into the universe and return to the all encompassing-ness of God after traversing all seven densities, with each of their eight octaves, composing the universe. Each density has eight octaves, according to the RA Material/Law of One.

    Oneness and perfection, coupled with is-now-ness and at-one-ment, are all that exist as the creation. This makes for another good breathing exercise. Breathe in oneness and exhale perfection. Breathe in is-now-ness and exhale at-one-ment. Continue to do so until your life becomes them. Perfection is the state when something exists as God's I Am-ness. Oneness is the relationship one has with itself as something that differs and, yet, is an aspect of one's life perfectly represented.

    This is misunderstood by most of humanity through denial, fear, guilt, and arrogance. These catalysts inherently prevent ascension if unresolved. They can be thought of as karma. Karma means unresolved issues and the accountability of negativity perpetrated. Perpetration reincarnates as its own victimization. This is why bad things happen to good people. It is why there is the idea of fate. We only meet those whom we are, as everyone who contributes to our life. This makes everyone a kind of soul mate. The ego only seeks to meet itself as the opposite of what it feels it is not. Our life is the union and oneness of mom and dad, and Yahweh and Id. These make us the human beings we are. This leaves God and universe to embrace and own as our life. Our entire life states what our reality and truth are through the experiences that correspond to what we feel, sense, think, and envision is who we are and why we are here.

Douglas H. Melloy

Part IV:

Path as Purpose

Invading the Indigenous while the Rest of Us Watch

The Ego

When we transition from our humanness into the realms beyond, we see our existence in a differing context, yet we are still tied to our idea or notion of being human. Those overly attached to hiser body and earthly life become ghosts. This is due to not knowing or thinking in terms of the soul. The body is a holograph of the mind. The spirit brings the body to life. The soul becomes conscious of itself as the body after the body is born and after the soul incarnates into the body. All things are a state of the mind. The universe is the state of God's mind. The body and all it experiences are representations of the mind. There is the holograph of the body, the holograph of what surrounds us, and the holograph of the universe. These are all representations of the same ideals. They are versions of God's I Am- ness that we humanize. Many mistake the ego as 'it.'

Our version makes it very manageable. Consciousness seeks to be the specific, while at the same time being the awareness of the universal-all encompassing- ness inversely reversed into the infinite, which shows us the diversification of God into all that is. We confuse our sense of identity with what is only a projection of the mind into third dimensional time and space. We then project from this, into our environment, what we feel is our reality, though it is not. This confusion is the death experience and all the dramas composing our life.

People have succeeded to a degree in remaking what is into versions of the ego. Staunchly, we hold onto our convictions. Blindly, we forge ahead, oblivious to our own creativity as the inner and outer experiences manifested according to our willed intention. God's will seeks to be and know only, and to remember Its true nature within what It is not. This works in conjunction with releasing. The art of letting go involves detachment and nonattachment to people, places, things, ideas, feelings, experiences, and states of consciousness. Within a medium that is infinite, absolutes cannot and do not exist. It is only the ego that seeks for and makes absolutes out of that which is impermanent. Nothing within the universe is an absolute, not even God. The ego is convinced otherwise. The ego is convinced that it alone is and exists. Traditions reinforce this fiction.

    We only come to know who we are, and then share that with others. Knowing the self is the path. How the self is shared with others is our purpose. This is like breathing. Going within is the path. Purpose is how that which is within is contributed to others. The application of attention through intention determines what transpires as our sharing our life with ourselves. This can be thought of as: "I am you, and you are me, and this is why we meet." Why is it my eyes never see themselves? It is curious to me that I never see my own face, only the face of others. The outer that surrounds my life as the environment and others is only a holographic projection of what is within me. It mirrors back to me what I feel and think is my life, humanly. The ego is expert in Da Vinci coding life into something sensible, yet untrue. Humanly, we do this through science, religion, politics, education, business, law, and medicine. We also do this through art, music, and just about everything else the ego deems is important.

    We cannot help ourselves. So fixated are we with our ego that we miss the point about everything else, like God, universe, reality, truth, love, and light. These ideas are usually completely beyond the realm of being and knowing personally, so they remain ideas of little or no merit. Again, the ego loves to make graven images of people who were misunderstood and ignored when they were alive, like Jesus and Buddha. What is the result of the Jewish people rejecting Jesus as their messiah? It is left to time to tell us. Eventually, it will. Hopefully, that failure will not be the end of the Jewish people as chosen. God never has a chosen people, because all people are the image and likeness of God existing as a human ideal. It is left to

Invading the Indigenous while the Rest of Us Watch

each of us to become God conscious that is then shared with others as a way-shower, deliverer, and healer.

Choice is all life is and avails us to make. We choose what we feel, think, and act. Most of what we choose is detrimental to this planet and each other. Many are out for hiser self. What is the relevance of a life that has passed on? Only what we make it out to be as what we aspire to through those who have come and died before us. Blindly, we refuse to question even the most obvious fabrications. So many believe the nonsense of the misbegotten. Arbitrarily, we entertain ourselves. People give value to insignificant ideals and things, thinking that those are the importance and meaning of life, when they are not. Individuality is confused by ideas conforming the lives of billions. "I am this, and I am that," we are told, over and over and over. Few own their uniqueness as a realized truth lived that pertains to what is as God and universe and all else, as self.

Meditation is the bane of many, for they do not engage in the practice. Meditation is how the path is walked within. It is self-awareness giving way to self-discovery. It is how 'what is' reveals itself to us when we are ready to be and know that as our life. Many do not resolve fear, so it prevents greater awareness and wisdom. Meditation is quieting the inner chaos into mindfulness and peaceful reflection. Sitting quietly allows what is to reveal itself to us within the timelessness of the moment. As we focus on our breathing, we discover "as within, so without," as well as, "as above, so below." That which continually draws our attention away from our inner being is the distraction that keeps us unaware and foreign to our true self and all it pertains to, humanly. Many do not realize addiction, dysfunction, and distraction are aspects of fear and denial. Many are too pained and afraid to look within. Within the quietude of silence rests the voice of God.

Humanity is left to itself to sort out its paradoxes of perplexity, lived as psychological states of mind. Experience involves both parties as the equation involving wholeness. Completeness seeks completeness. This is the unification of what is with itself, humanly. The art of movement is change. Change is the continual desire for all that is to become one state of existence. This is accomplished, on one level, through ascension. Individuality is the infiniteness of God existing as I Am-ness. All aspects of the creation seek for one thing, the return to God as God. Movement as change allows God to become Itself once again through experience and evolution. This is the infinitesimal becoming the universal, which becomes all encompassing. Everything in the universe is doing this, moment by moment, through experience. From God, through God, to God, as God is the creation and is what ascension culminates in through unification of differing states into one that is ongoing.

Awareness acts like concentric circles. As it becomes conscious of itself, the holograph of self enlarges. Awareness extends and expands itself through applied attentive intention. This process works in two ways, inwardly and outwardly. This is called depth of being and scope of knowing. True enlightenment is only possible when both God as the very small and the universe as the very large are embraced as what they are, humanly. God consciousness is only possible when the universe is known and owned as one's own soul. The all encompassing-ness of God is balanced with the infinitude of all that is. There is only equality, balance, relationship, purpose, , and harmony between God and universe, existing as our human being- ness, which are mind and soul.

Awareness goes inward and outward evenly and equally. When 'all that is' is known as the soul, one also comes face-to-face with God as That is, where it is. This means that awareness travels in two directions at the same time. This is like traveling inside a globe to the center of the globe and its circumference. In between these two points of reference is awareness. The center is positive and the circumference is negative, while awareness is neutral. From this perspective, the choice is made to either control or create energy. Controlling energy is the negative path. Creating energy is the positive path. Creativity requires the conscious use of God's will while living love and light. Those who serve the negative path do not have the ability of creating anything consciously. The choice we are all given divides between destroying and creating.

Invading the Indigenous while the Rest of Us Watch

Effective creativity heals the death experience and culminates in collective ascension.

Another contrast to our human experience is living according to either being in possession of or taking possession of what is, through our intention of purpose. The ego is only interested in getting from people its needs and wants met. Ownership is the goal of those who "take possession of. "This establishes the syndrome of the king and queen, as well as the fact of the nation state. It is also the basis for the establishment of cities and towns, which are versions of Sodom and Gomorrah. It is also the basis for gender disparity and inequality between people. The art of acquisition requires giving arbitrary value to land, people, and artifacts. These are then paraded for the rest of the world to see, the question always being, is my ego big enough to win? Self-glorification is a precursor to the negative path of serving the ego by taking possession of what becomes one's little kingdom. How many of the rich and famous exemplify a life similar to that of Jesus or Buddha? The sad fact is that no one does. It is like the rich and famous embody Sodom and Gomorrah as a class. Always, we are brought back to what contribution we are making to others through our life as the reality shared truthfully.

The success of those who "take possession of" begins with false doctrine used to persuade people into following and obeying without questioning. Many do this now within the context of nation, tradition, and ideology. People identify themselves as race, family, education, career, talents, issues, gender, country, circumstances, conditions, experiences, and attitudes. These catalysts either blind or bind, or they assist us with our evolution in growing beyond them. Our outer sense of identity, the ego, is not our true identity. The outer mirroring back to us is a projection of what is within us. This is how we actually 'see' ourselves. Then, we either embrace this as our life, or we reject it. These are the roles that acceptance and judgment play as what we feel and think. It is also the basis for why forgiveness and judgment are ideas we apply ourselves to.

Free will lends itself to living arbitrarily. We are each given the opportunity to choose what is so about anything and everyone.

Douglas H. Melloy

Why people choose to be unfriendly and antagonistic is curious and odd. We are all cartoon characters in the mind of God. Nothing is the same, yet people conform themselves to points of reference that are meaningless and irrelevant to the nature of the self. The self is the soul evolving love/light forever as a state of consciousness. To understand this requires a working knowledge of what composes one's identity as a holograph of the mind, coupled with the awareness that one is a person on a planet within an ongoing universe. The nature of the self is not easy to fathom or grasp. Also not easy to resolve is the paradox of individuality and collectivity-the partial view within what is universal.

Expanding one's point of view is not easy, for it requires letting go of ideas that make our biology what it is. Disengaging from the ego's insistence that the body is it and only it exists is not easy. The ego is our sense of time and space, nothing more. It gives us our sense of duration and placement within a specified ideal. The ego allows for the experience and expression of what is into something specific and personal, like God and universe. The curiosity of our experience is how people relate to what is beyond their awareness. Usually, expanded awareness is discounted and denied, yet there is a direct correspondence between the ideas involving and regarding the existence of this that we refuse to embrace, own, and live.

Death is the distance between what we died and the reality of our existence. Ascension is the is-now-ness of God, existing as a presented awareness that evolves service into eternal continuance through our willingness to humanize God and universe according to this planet.

This is the dance of being. It encompasses all that is, as well as that which gave rise to it, from a context that is arbitrary as intentionally designed. We exist as we do because this is how we were created to live, idealistically. Humanly, we identify Yahweh, Id, mom, and dad. These correspond to heart, head, the feminine, and the masculine unified into a single ideal. Again, the heart is Yahweh, the head is Id, the feminine is mom, and the masculine is dad. These are the fourfold natures of being composing the unified field theory

Invading the Indigenous while the Rest of Us Watch

as self. Woman is the inverse reversal of man, just as our parents are the inverse reversal of our creator and bestower. All opposites exist through the technique of inverse reversal. This establishes binary vibrancy, which is also the pulse of God. Pulsation is what makes holographs representations of the mind of God. It is our blueprint, recorded as our DNA. People need to stop coining ideas just to make money and become famous, and to stop regurgitating information just to sell books. Money is the symbol of greed. It is also the icon of power. It is the false god of the self-serving. It is a form of ego. It is false identity giving rise to false ideology and idol worship. Money is the means whereby the ego becomes glorified and worshiped. It is the means whereby the ego is made superior to others. Money establishes the ideal of being elite. All for the sake of class distinction and self-idolization.

Every external version of God is the ego trying to disguise itself as the false god worshipped. It is only the ego that demands worship as a ritualized practice. Rituals are the fear the ego holds onto until death. Ego is the face of fear and death. It is the mask worn by the body that is a holograph of the mind, which is God's human form and identity. This is something missed by almost everyone. The inherent becomes the apparent, which is then shared with others humbly and transparently. This is the path of serving others through conscious contribution. The mechanics involved with path as purpose are our arbitrariness. Others must have a greater importance than we give ourselves because others have a greater significance than we do, individually. Greater and lesser do not exist within a medium that is infinite. "Making a contribution to" is the only point of relevance involving and concerning others. We are all extensions and expansions of each other and what is. Everything composing the universe is the extension and expansion of God into all that is. This is the infinitude of God's all encompassing-ness into self-expression as experience, which is either feared or enjoyed.

Small-minded pursuits are the arbitrariness of the ego, which is also the scripted encoding of the blueprint of the soul prior to its incarnation. Attachment is the addiction the ego has about itself to the objects of its desire. These can be anything or anyone the ego finds attractive to its objectification of itself as idol worship. It is curious-all the ideas people entertain about the objectification of fear into a threatening god, demon, or boogey man. Then, people do something insane; they try to appease their fear through worship and prayer. It is like people are asking God to protect them from their fearful imagination. The irony is that unresolved fear and selfishness, acting as the ego, is the death experience. It is this, and this alone, that we are healing.

    Nuance is the name of the game. It is the basis of uniqueness and individuality. We are each entitled to living our life as we choose to, humanly. Likes and dislikes are our arbitrariness exposed. Eating, drinking, and what we wear have nothing to do with the path and how it is shared with others. Those who think that they do are misguided. Externals are outer versions of what we feel and think about our basic nature. God and health are states of our mind. The body simply represents them humanly. Nothing one does adds to or distracts from what love and light are as our embodied spirituality. The idea that one is becoming more spiritual is pure nonsense. Notice how people never claim to be striving towards becoming more physical. There is only the equality, balance, relationship, purpose, and harmony between love as the physical and light as the spiritual that we live as our body and spirit. We are also the mind of God and the soul of the universe, humanly. The key to living humanly is the equality and balance between love and light and fear and darkness. It is impossible to add to or detract from what we are physically and spiritually. One is not greater or lesser than the other. They simply represent love and light humanly as male and female unified as the masculine and feminine we each are.

    The beauty of this design is exquisite! All is in divine order as the perfection it is, existing as what is appropriate for each one of us. Who we are meets us where we stand. We only come face to face as whom we are by our life being shown to us through others. It is how we see the what's so about ourselves, daily. Sometimes, what presents itself can be unpleasant and quite disturbing. Some forms of

Invading the Indigenous while the Rest of Us Watch

negativity experienced take lifetimes to resolve. The interpretations we give stop us for a while until we get over ourselves as that. People fascinate me who hold onto figments of their imagination, as if they were real and true, to such an extent that their lives become nothing but the habitualized rituals of fear and ignorance called the human condition of drama. What does it take to evolve beyond the human condition? Faith, desire, and determination through intention and the attention one gives to healing affliction and lower levels of consciousness.

******

The physical that we live as our body and the spiritual that we live as our identity are states of love and light, humanized. Love is the body as the physical. Light is the spirit as our spirituality. These are fixed. One no more adds to hiser physical body than he or she does to hiser spirituality. One only becomes more conscious of what he or she is as love and light. This requires healing fear and darkness as predominators of one's life as the ego. It is like our life is neutral. We then get to choose what we are, humanly, as either what is positive or negative, which is then shared with others. Service polarity is what ascends. This is making the conscious decision to contribute to others as the self-serving or as one who serves others. This is self-idealization, or collective consciousness. These can be thought of as self-idolization or Christ consciousness. The positive path is how one resolves hiser negative side or nature. The negative path is how love and light are denied and feared. It is how false gods come into existence, like Jehovah.

To the average person, neither the positive nor negative path is considered. One's life is lived as something arbitrary. The focus is usually small-minded pursuits. The art is the conformity of fitting in. The ego only seeks to fit in and belong. One rarely ventures outside or beyond typical expectations. The outer reflects back the accepted norms of tradition and beliefs. This always leads to life outliving us and evolving beyond us. We are buried, and then go to where we believe we do as the 'end' of our existence. For some, it is the heaven of their own making. Energy conforms itself to our ways of feeling and thinking. This is why we are told, "We create our own reality."The life we exist as, humanly, demonstrates for all to see what our blueprint is as our experience. This is the common denominator between us and those with whom we interact daily. Some play the role of the antagonist, while others play the role of the teacher. These assist us in healing issues and developing talents into a way of life that is meaningful and rewarding, as well as challenging to us.

The ego always seeks for an absolute to attain that is 'it.' Those who truly know understand that any insight or experience is only an aspect of a greater reality and truth, eternally. Ends are only the beginning, which become more conscious infinitely, and there is never an end to eternity and self-realization, which is continuously evolving into larger states of being, knowing, sharing, and ascending, This requires moving one's awareness beyond the ego and its self-absorption. Critical to the path is going it alone for as long as it takes to heal and live a life of serving others, though not by denying one's physical life for esoteric ideals, where self is either martyred or sacrificed. According to the RA Material/Law of One, the path of serving others is 49 percent self and 51 percent contributing to others. For those who serve themselves, the breakdown is 95 percent self and 5 percent others. These determine which path is served. Both involve the same amount of effort.

Individuality has as much a right to exist negatively as positively as a chosen polarity. Service is what evolves. Individuality in its truest context does not exist. Understanding this requires a working knowledge of the universe and the role individuality plays. In and of itself, individuality is an illusion thought of as the ego. It is the mask or face of the body, which is a holograph of the mind. It is our spirituality that makes us believe we are our individuality, living and existing independent of all else. Reconciliation is necessary for us, allowing all that we are to be the humanness we are now here being. Lacking this, the ego will dominate our life to the death.

Invading the Indigenous while the Rest of Us Watch

Arbitrariness is the decision-making process of the ego that only relies upon externals for what it believes and places its faith in. This will be people, places, and things, coupled with the emotions, thoughts, and interests one holds to, humanly. The ego does this because it is always seeking to get from what it places significance with involving external sources of interest.

Arbitrariness is a curious way we live humanly. Anything goes. People, places, and things are given significance and meaning through the ego. The ego only thinks in terms of absolutes through exclusion, negation, and aversion. This is the exclusion of God, the negation of life, and the aversion of others. The ego has replaced these with itself. It has established traditions to ensure nothing replaces it except death. The ego demands proof, for in and of itself it is nothing. The body is the effect of the mind, and the ego is the effect of the body. This means we are double blind in our trying to make sense of anything, which is why very little, humanly, makes any sense at all to us now. It is also why so much disinformation exists currently. The sad irony is that many have sold out to their ego. All for the sake of being glorified and idolized, making an famous name for him or herself.

The ego does allow us to identify with and relate to others, sort of. The ego is primarily concerned with what is a threat to its existence, and what it can get from others. This means it has to hold to fear and control for it to feel safe from itself. This methodology reinforces its point of view rather than healing it. Satan is another name for the ego's fear. God, as something worshipped and obeyed, is another name for the ego's denial. The ego likes to stick and carrot itself until it dies. This is done through the myths of past, present, and future. The past is all the ideas the ego holds onto as the way it once was. The future is a subjective way of thinking what might become according to the past. This is why the death experience takes place. The present divides between what is past or what might be, so the now is missed entirely as to what it is as real and true as one's self. The ego only identifies with tangibles it considers to be its life here, based on the body as 'it,' the only thing that exists. Tangibles make the ego feel it is real and alive. They give the ego a sense of identity and belonging. Ownership is the ego thinking it has something of value, giving credibility to its nothingness. People, places, and things only exist so the ego can feel it is something of importance and valuable. The art of the ego is conquering, enslaving, and destroying. It is the basis for the negative path of the invader culture. The invader culture is only made possible through the ego and the attention it gives to externals masquerading as "the one true God."

How well does my sense of identity work, involving and regarding the opposite sex, society, and this planet? This leaves God and universe to account for, humanly. If left to the ego to answer that question, we get life as it is lived by most of humanity--lots of insane ideas that are misguided and ungrounded. We are convinced we are correct about our insanity. Ah, the arrogance of our foolishness. The obvious acts more like a tombstone than a way of deliverance. To the Christian, I ask, is your faith religiously to avoid Hell? If so, then your faith is one of avoidance only, not entering the kingdom of Love/Light as love/light. Spirituality is not determined by what we drink, eat, and wear. Experience is the only measure by which a given state has any human validity. Experience is the expression of what we embody humanly. It is the only measure by which what we feel and think is known to us as our reality and truth. It can be anything at all. What does a person desire hiser life to be, know, and share?

People are drawn to their soul's blueprinting. We observe the lives of others and tell ourselves that this is the way our life is supposed to be, so our lives become that, and we live happily ever after, of course, or so we think. Then, something negative comes along and bursts our bubble. We are devastated. Recovery is not easy. For some, they never get over it. The wise ones use this as an opportunity for growth in wisdom and humility. The victim blames the perpetrator. The perpetrator only serves the purpose the role is designed for-- to assist the victim in hiser evolution. People do not get what two plus two actually means as involved experience.

Existence is like concentric circles acting as holographic projections of differing magnitudes, beginning with the body, then

Invading the Indigenous while the Rest of Us Watch

planet, and finally, universe. There are many more than just three. Always, I am brought back to the human element with an idea. How does this idea involve and pertain to my human being-ness? Often the ideas we believe in do not pertain to anything; they are just information to keep us preoccupied and distracted. I remember reading a book where, after 135 pages, only five sentences stated something, so I tore it up and burned it! Many books are like that. The only truth of any relevance is, are you going to ascend, taking your body with you when you go? The answer for most of humanity is no. Why not? People do not know how to ascend. They are stuck egoically. Almost everyone teaching today is not going to ascend. It is not an aspect of their blueprint. Wishful thinking will not do it. The ego is incapable of deciding whether one will live or die. Death is an aspect of one's blueprint.

Understanding requires experience to make sense and to be applicable to others. Lacking experience, nothing makes sense or has any relevance. Rarely do we put people and their life and teachings in the first person, so that their life and ours make sense. We are the image and likeness of God, humanly. This includes all of existence, from God to universe, and everything in between. Evolving beyond the human condition requires letting go of the ego as a predominator and allowing 'what is to become one's life. This is not easy, especially for people who are wealthy, famous, and in positions of power. The ego is so identified with by most people that resolving it is the last thing they aspire to accomplish. People are addicted to the adulations of others, so that the ego is treated like a false god. Idol worship, from gods to ego, is the downfall of all who pass on. Only the ego feels it needs to be worshipped. God certainly does not. Those who are true to serving others as love and light do not. The creator and bestower of humanity do not. Only that which is selfish does. Only those who are superstitious worship self-serving imaginations of the projected as something of importance. This is a common denominator for many people. The outer is confused as the way it is and what is, when it is not. It is the ego that makes this mistake in awareness.

Douglas H. Melloy

Contrast is essential, for only then is something known for what it is, as it is. Free will is the way of existence. It is a universal law of conduct. It is the basis for how people live humanly. It is arbitrary, and anything goes because of it. We are free to live as we choose. This is by design and intention. Violating free will is a no-no and against universal law. Both sides in the development of consciousness honor free will. The only way that those who are service polarized can have any affect on us is for us to believe their point of application. Anyone who refuses to believe the intentions of another, earth bound or from outer space, is off limits to that individual. It is only in belief that one is affected by what the belief is in. People have to believe in what is posited in order to become involved with the agenda behind the ideology. This catches many unaware. Blind belief in ideologies is what the self-serving need to be successful with enslaving people to the grave.

This art form involves conquering through ideology, like religion or science, then enslavement, and finally destroying, which is the death experience. Death is only possible when life is denied its existence according to the individual who dies. Death is only possible through the ego and its attachment to fear. The ego is fearful unto the death. Love is lived as the self that ascends, after love is shared through purpose. The inner path is choosing to be love and know light, which is then shared with others humbly and transparently. Those who are false prophets always have an agenda that is kept secret from those who become the faithful. People place their faith in ideals that oftentimes are misguided. Faith is then misplaced. The irony of existence is that energy conforms itself to whatever beliefs we choose to feel and think. Heaven and hell are what we make them out to be for us. There is never an end to what the universe will be for us as an ongoing place of involvement. Just as our life is down here, so it is as our continued experience up there.

Invading the Indigenous while the Rest of Us Watch

Evolution, Negativity, and Balance

What is the nature of the soul, and where does it come from? The soul is to the universe what the body is to earth. Just as the mind is to God what the spirit is to life. To know one's own soul is to be consciously aware of both the role the body plays and that of the soul within two differing mediums of experience, the universe and the planet. Why are there differing states of awareness, like body and soul? It is infinity that gives God I Am-ness. The natural tendency for a given aspect of the universe is to remain as-is indefinitely, so there is an agency in place that breaks energy down as the death experience in order that consciousness, as the soul, can continue to evolve back into what gave rise to it. This is the returning of God, as the specific, back into Its original state of existence. This is a twofold ascension process firstly, ascending from a planetary state of being and knowing and then from a universal state of being and knowing, back into God.

God is an idea that is meant to inspire a sense of reverence and to be a unifying principle. Many miss this point, thinking of God in terms that are more egotistical than actual. Many of the various gods worshipped by people are versions of the ego, nothing more. Many are forms of negativity idolized and worshipped. The only idea for God that works for me is all encompassing-ness. Any other idea places a limitation on God. God is all that is, including every one of us. Everything in existence, including the universe, is a state of God being that, solely for the experience of it. The universe is God experiencing infinity as a diversification of all encompassing-ness. Infinity means variable and variety of that which remains constant. God is the constancy that never changes.

Change is the evolution of God back into Itself through experience and intention. God only seeks the unification of Itself into oneness. This is accomplished through ascension, either individually or collectively. People ignore collective consciousness by seeking ideals that are absolute, like bliss, nirvana, or perfection. Within a medium that is infinite, absolutes do not exist, ever. God as a state is only recognized as a collective, not as an absolute. Even when God's original state is entered into, it is not absolute. It is within a diversity of states lived as a human being. Human beingness is a collection of diversified states that are unified, along with the oneness of them, into an ideal that represents what they are within a planetary medium. This allows for one to become effective in either creativity or control through a path of service that is one's purpose lived through contribution.

Anyone that is not living hiser life as the service polarized is living an arbitrary life as chaff on this planet. It is only service polarity that has the potential for ascension, as it is only these that evolve. Positive service polarity requires a working knowledge of the Christ as one's own life and of humanity as a whole. Understanding equality, balance, relationship, purpose, and harmony are also very useful. Class distinction and gender disparity must end before the Christ will return to this planet as the humanity that inhabits it. Anyone who lives contrary to what earth is, as an embodied spirituality, will not survive the earth giving birth to a new version of itself as a new ideal. This will be a positive ideal based that kind of energy. This means letting go of negativity as a point of view. Not easy to do, as we are addicted to negativity and its basic nature of fear through the ego. We are addicted to our ego and the dysfunctions that accompany it.

Individuality plays its part, but there is also the relational and social. Coupled with this are the planetary and the universal. All play a role. We are involved with all five simultaneously. We ignore most of them to such an extent that they do not make any sense to us personally. We leave the wisdom of the cosmos to science and the existence of God to religion. I hold to the beliefs that science is designed to deny the existence of God, and religion's intention is teaching false doctrines about God. Both have succeeded very

Invading the Indigenous while the Rest of Us Watch

well in confusing people about God's life- humanly, globally, and universally. One day, we will get it, but not before most of humanity has perished, becoming extinct.

I am very curious how many people will survive to continue the evolution of our species until it collectively ascends as the Christ. Some believe we all will. Others believe only the faithful will. There are those who think only 144,000 will be chosen. Another view is that humanity is headed for extinction through either pollution or nuclear war. I suppose there are as many views about what comes as there are people who live here. What is our correspondence? It is our biology that is the same as that of this planet. The same love and light that is the creation, as this planet, is our embodied spirituality. We are responsible for being and knowing these as the life we are living. Most of humanity refuses to embrace love as the body, and light as the spirit, also will as the mind and universe as the soul.

Life as and on this planet eventually evolves beyond lower levels of existence. This is most of what composes modern day living within cities and nations. The irrelevant, that we insist upon personifying, will become extinct, as it has nothing to do with realness and truth as life. Those clinging to what is untenable will find they have faded away forever. People are given as long as they need to get it and evolve. How many lifetimes will it take you to ascend, taking your body with you when you go? All depends on the work to which one applies him or herself. Many are lifetimes away from the possibility of ascension. Only those who are left behind will continue the evolution of us until we collectively ascend as the Christ through the love of Yahweh and the light of Id. Again, our biological parents are the inverse reversal of this. Making sense of our humanness requires understanding the roles of divinity and deity and the masculine and feminine. These are lived as our heart and head, and as our feminine and masculine natures.

These are the four points of the true cross. The center of the cross is where God resides. What surrounds the cross is consciousness. The cross looks like a plus sign, where both parts are equal in length. There is only equality and balance between mom and dad, and Yahweh and Id. Why people do not understand and live this is curious. Our reality is not that difficult to understand and own, and then share with others with a smile; it only takes desire and diligence in being what these are here and now as one's human being-ness. Arbitrariness and free will allow for us to feel, think, and experience anything we desire to. Anything. It is our divine right to explore experience so we know what energy feels like as that. It is the nature of curiosity. Having this attitude, the life another lives is pointless and meaningless. Only the life we are being and sharing means anything. From my perspective, I do not know what is actually going on with another in and as hiser life. Taking sides means I have missed the point. Making a judgment about another means I have failed in my relationship to myself as the life he or she is experiencing. All one can do is love, accept, and remain even-minded about the lives of others, and under all circumstances.

The advice we were given by Jesus was to love, forgive, and do unto others. Doing unto others is serving others as ourselves. If we truly lived this one idea as the love we are, "Thou shalt not" would not be needed. Love is God, the relationship God has with Its I Am-ness, and what everything within the creation is created as and through. Why we focus on fear is curious. Actually it does not make any sense at all. Yet, almost all of humanity is convinced that fear and darkness are the reality, rather than love and light. Energy, as the positive and negative, is unified into a neutral state. This state then polarizes into either what serves others or what serves the ego. This is how consciousness evolves humanly. Again, making a contribution is the only measure by which one's life gives value and meaning within the creation. Many do not understand this very well, if at all.

I often wonder what famous people face during their whole-life review. I am sure it is a surprise to them. What kinds of karma do they have to resolve? What is the atonement for ideas that lead many astray? How many lifetimes will it take to balance out one's karma? God only knows. Always be honest and kind to others. This way, very little will affect one's life karmically. Thinking of others

Invading the Indigenous while the Rest of Us Watch

as an extension of one's life makes service easy. I am you and you are I and this is why we meet is the advice that makes contribution easy, especially with people whose role is that of the petty tyrant. People who hold onto the ills of their past fascinate me. The ills of the past always become the blessings of the present when we resolve them. Catalysts are inherent. They come with us when we come to life. Everyone has issues acting as triggers for growth and wisdom. It is how we evolve into greater levels of being shared.

Many resist delving into their issues of pain, fear, anger, jealousy, and the like, which is necessary to understand what purpose each catalyst serves their life. Many tell me they are unwilling to do this, yet pain makes itself known anyway, as does fear and all the catalysts afflicting us. Then, we do something naïve; we believe heaven is completely different. It is not! "As above, so below" tells us that up there is no different than down here. Christians have a hard go- with this truth. They are convinced that following blindly takes them to a place that is completely different than their life down here. Nothing could be farther from the truth. Anything unresolved during their life will have to be resolved in another life. Death is ultimately what we resolve--into life that ascends. Taking the body with it is how a life lived is measured. Anyone leaving hiser body behind will have to reincarnate again. This is the fact of evolution. The body is love made manifest. Just as the spirit is light identified. These are our embodied spirituality.

The invader culture mindset is coming to an end. Humanity will return to living as designed. It is time for the rest of us to go home. Third density is ending. Fourth density is about to be born. Now is the time of harvest. The positive aspect of this only involves those who have chosen to serve others. Religious faith is irrelevant as it does not establish one's relationship to God-love does. Love is the life we are being, humanly, as our body. Death is fear held as the ego. In order for humanity to evolve and ascend, everyone must be heart based, rather than stuck in the head. It is in the heart that connection is made and where God resides. Change is the evolution required for God to return to Itself. God incarnates into Itself as what It is not. This is what ascends through experience as expressed. This is only possible when consciousness knows what God is as the self. It is evolving beyond individuality, opposites in conflict, and selfishness. Ends are only the beginning of something new and, hopefully, more evolved.

Evolution is the change consciousness makes as what it believes it is. This is from something fear-based into the realness of love and light, humanly portrayed as both male and female. Each of us is the union and oneness of man and woman as the masculine and feminine. Humanly, we are also the union and oneness of divinity and deity. These four states make us human beings that know, share, and ascend. Ascension is the pinnacle of evolution's achievement. It is literally the changing of love and light as the biological into what is eternal in nature. This requires being love and knowing light as one's humanness, and being this requires meditation to accomplish. People who do not meditate do not know who they are or what they are communicating to others. Meditation and intuition are the keys to knowing the real that is true as it pertains to our life. There is always a direct correlation to our life and how it pertains to God and universe as our identity.

The negative engagements of society make this impossible to be and know. The positive elements of humanity always encourage us to love and serve others. The arbitrary ways of being and knowing mean that anything goes. The human ideal very well. Everyone is responsible for what he or she feels, thinks, and acts upon. We are entitled to our life as we live it. Nuance is the name of the game. We have to decide when differences are not more important than what gets along, humanly, with people, biology, and differing life forms. "Taking possession of" is the ideology of ownership. "Being in possession of" is what is truly contributed to others. There are those who take. There are those who give. There are those of us who give and take. The line of demarcation between them and us is often blurred. Chuang Tzu stated, "You are not me, I am not you." I rephrased this into, "You are me and I am you, and this is why we meet." Not easy to see or understand, due to our ego and

Invading the Indigenous while the Rest of Us Watch

to our being stuck with the belief that we are separated from each other. The ego only seeks to get from others and the environment. Nothingness seeking to get something it considers valuable and having significance and some kind of importance.

    Before the path as purpose can begin, one has to go it alone for a season or two. This requires leaving everything and everyone behind. (I have done this several times, and am currently doing it again. I am living in an area where there is no family, no friends, no relationship, no job, no money--just my dog, cat, and me. This allows me to be undistracted with myself to see who I am as what I feel and think. It has been this way for nine months. I feel like I am in a womb. I have made a few significant changes where I currently live. My focus centers on a few ideas and some ideals. Faith, patience, and allowing are essential for my life to become my intentions.) The art of going it alone is not easy. Many are not comfortable being alone with just the self. But periods of "the dark night of the soul" are very beneficial to healing, wisdom, and comfort-ability.

    How comfortable do we feel in and with our own skin? Many do not like who they are. Some elements despise and hate who and what we are, humanly. Case in point: the warlord god Jehovah. To that entity, we are an abomination. The invader culture lives as it does to hate, war against, and disenfranchise almost all of humanity. Its role is to keep people steeped in fear, guilt, arrogance, and denial. Chosen-ness and good versus evil are its battle cry. This false god is 'good,' as are its chosen people, and everyone else is considered evil, necessitating judgment and persecution. Humanness has been converted into death through the various false doctrines people worship and obey. Life was converted into death. All who die have chosen to do this just to fit in and not offend that which hates our humanity, which is the warlord god Jehovah, which is a god that demands we fear it, worship it, obey it, and die for it. All under the premise it is "the one true God."

Single-minded myopia is all we have accomplished through the various beliefs revered and perpetuated. Nothing has changed in eleven thousand years. Humanity still lives the afflictions of war, selfishness, and death. These are what we are here to evolve beyond by no longing holding onto what they are, as forms of psychology only. These are states of the mind that we embody, that the spirit brings to life, and of which the soul becomes conscious as its identity in human form. This is true of everything we feel and think. They are states of mind that become the body as our spirituality that is ensouled. The work we do in consciousness is becoming aware of why we feel as we do and letting go of everything that hinders our evolution--our collective ascension. This is not easy to do, humanly, as we are focused on so many things that keep us from getting along and feeling good about our life.

The art of contrariness is the art of selfishness. Everything we live is a learned behavior. We pattern ourselves after our parents, friends, or peers we admire. This is coupled with our soul's blueprint. These determine our internal and external lives. It is like we are living a 'split' personality, because we have connected with the external world as an extension and expansion of our basic nature. Making this connection integrates our inner being with our outer knowing, which is lived as a unified reality. This reestablishes peace within and environmental harmony, all emanating from a state of stillness. Faith, trust, certainty, confidence, and clarity are all that is required for true success, humanly. Walking away from conflict is part of the path. Process resolution of emotional causation is a big part of what life affords us to accomplish. This is looking at what is felt and asking what purpose it serves our life. When one knows the answer, healing comes, as the catalyst, acting as what is resolved, is no longer needed. This is the role everything negative plays for us. It is to evolve beyond limitations of confusion. This is also the role the ego plays. The ego is the mask of the body, which is a holograph of the mind that the spirit brings to life. These are what the soul becomes conscious of as its sense of being and identity on this planet.

Invading the Indigenous while the Rest of Us Watch

Ascension

      Mindful purposefulness is one of the roles we get to assume. This is coupled with embodied spirituality and conscious awareness, as the path and purpose of serving others. These are the precursors to ascension. Holding to the ego as one's entire life is like holding to a grain of sand or a dot. What is ignored is the rest of the picture of creation. This also can be thought of as time and space. It is only the ego, as an entity unto itself, that convinces us time and space exist. Time is the duration of the ego. Space is the placement of the ego. Letting go of the what dominates our life, is part of the path, as is letting go of the idea our body is 'it.' Ascension is our evolution beyond the ego/body as an absolute of glorified idolization. Anything worshipped as an external idol means we have missed the point entirely about our life as what exists. What is missed is the nature of holographic structure, which is God within the heart; the heart; the torso; the head; this planet; and the universe. These are what we become mindful about through meditation and focused breathing. Humanness is the union and oneness of God, planet, and universe into a single ideal.
      Expansion is all consciousness does through attention and intention as mindful purposefulness that is shared with others transparently. False gods come and go, historically. Each aspires to become identical to the warlord god Jehovah. Many are successful in creating empires of disrepute within many mediums to which people contribute emotionally and financially. All miss the mark, for they represent the mark of the beast. It is always an external symbol. Take any symbol used to represent an organization that is the mark of the beast. True symbols are always organic, and they correspond to what is natural, like the sun, earth, moon, or galaxy. I suspect

scared geometry is the wisdom of the self-serving, but then, what do I know? Nothing.

This insight makes me laugh. How does a given insight allow for greater wisdom to come? Usually, what is believed is considered 'it' by many. Everything in existence evolves into greater levels of being, knowing, and sharing. Everything eventually evolves back into God. This requires that it evolve into differing forms of expression. There is also the law of attraction, which draws love and light into what collectively ascends. All forms of conflict and competition have to be resolved before this will happen. Everything is the extension and expansion of God through form and function. Forms never cease to evolve into greater levels of being and knowing. It is our addictive nature that hinders or prevents greater levels of awareness and application. Also, it is our insistence on distracting our attention away from what we are as what we feel and think..
Humanity is returning to its original design and intention. In order to do so, all forms of false identity must cease to exist. The second coming is our returning to connection with each other, this planet, and the biology composing life. Artificial ways of intelligence are becoming extinct now. The family of humanity will bring the Christ back when everyone is living love and light as their embodied spirituality that is shared. This requires ending fear as our death experience. My masculine and feminine sides are biased as the male. This is a type of role-playing only. It is the same for a woman, through the technique of inverse reversal. Her feminine and masculine sides are biased as the female. Sexuality unifies man and woman into the oneness of being. This is not understood very well now. There is only equality and balance between divergent states on many levels.

The universe has seven primary levels to it. Secondary to this are fifty-six sub- states. The breakdown from here is endlessness. Then, we do something very interesting, humanly; we decide to discount, ignore, judge, and refute nonegoic states of awareness and being. We only believe what our eyes see and our intellect deduces as what is possible and the way it is because a given state

Invading the Indigenous while the Rest of Us Watch

can be proven to exist according to our interpretation of what it is. How does proof allow for change? One might answer, 'Evolution.' Curiously, we all are expected to believe in the same ideas about what is observed. The irony of this is that no two people observe something in the same way. No two perspectives are identical, so no one sees something as the same from hiser perspective. Another oddity with people is their choosing to believe the same ideas about someone's interpretation. Individually, we come to be and know our own reality and truth; we then share these, as our path as purpose, through what we contribute to others. The choice made is something personal. Hopefully, one's choice of purpose is that of the soul, not of the expectations of others.

Oftentimes, the family one is born into is the antithesis of one's true purpose in life, and it takes asking the question and listening for the answer to come, intuitively. I knew at a young age that I would be a teacher. Accepting one's lot in life is also important. Many try to be everything they are not. It is like we refuse to own our humanness for all kinds of nonsensical points of view. People think they are their occupation, their body, their psychology, the stuff' they own, money, people they know, and their accomplishments. What is ignored and left out are all the other aspects making us the humans we are. Death is like the disparity between what we believed ourselves to be and what we actually are as God, planet, and universe. To know these as the self requires a working knowledge of mind, body, spirit, and soul. The ego will deny and fear these to the death.

People need to reconnect consciously with what is integrated as their life. This is done, consciously, through seeking to be and know the self humanly. The evolution of knowing the self is the path. Purpose is how this is shared with others, humbly. The culmination of the experience is ascension, either singly or collectively. Again, individual ascension is more negative than positive. Collective ascension is always positive. There is more to life than just us. Individually, we are insignificant to the greater whole. This is true of anyone. The Christ is the collective consciousness of humanity as a unified whole. It is never an individual, like Jesus. The Christ consciousness is the third chakra. It is only the ego that makes Jesus into someone he is not.

It is only our arbitrariness that prevents us from being able to identify with greater levels of awareness and with social practices that are more universal than happenstance. We remain confused and insane by holding onto ideas that are propaganda only. Even this is propaganda to see what you'll believe. That statement needs to be the disclaimer at the end of everything we read, watch, observe, or hear. Intuition is the voice of truth that speaks to us quietly when we are calm, peaceful, and willing to listen to it. The outer keeps us distracted and convinced that only what it presents to us is valid. Never mind that outer-based sources are not our reality or truth in being, knowing, and making a contribution to others. Believing in what others feel is the ideal only keeps us from owning our truth, which is the only truth that is valid as one's life.

The cliffs of the lemmings are many. I remember reading somewhere that humanity was given two thousand years to end war, greed, and class distinction on this planet after the time of Jesus' teachings. People have refused to let go of what is untenable humanly. People are addicted to their negativity. People are more interested in death than in living life as it exists. Living life requires knowing what we are as biological planetary beings. It is like life is passing us by now.

Great change is in the air. We feel something profound is going to happen. We look around, hoping to see what it is before it gets us. All kinds of ideas are posited about who we are and why we are here. For those of us who are interested in knowing what aspect of this planet was used in our creation as human beings, look no farther than the Lemur. This is according to the RA Material.

The time of the harvesting of souls is at hand. The invader culture mindset will become extinct. Those who are not harvested will repeat third density elsewhere. The planet will have to be similar to this one. I was told the conditions possible for this will not be for ten million years. The 'source' added that this was a blink

Invading the Indigenous while the Rest of Us Watch

of an eye. Details are often missed about what is so, as it involves our humanity and its evolution beyond the biological and planetary. We have disconnected from our heart and treat our body as if is alien to this planet. People are oblivious to what is natural. Artificial intelligence blinds us and dazzles us into oblivion. Walking away from the grid is considered insane and pure folly. Restoration is what is happening, not the end of the world. Ends only involve what is untenable in the reality that becomes life on this planet, according to the density now being birthed, which is fourth density. This is like giving birth to a new identity of connected integration through letting go of one's false identity, the ego.

What makes us a human being is the only question we ever answer. Answering it requires being human. Humanity is reestablishing its natural connectedness to this planet as the biology we are. It is not about becoming more spiritual. It is living the love and light that makes us the image and likeness of God according to Yahweh and Id. Our parents are the inverse reversal of our creator and the bestower. Opposites do not make sense to us because we do not know what inverse reversal is, as holographic ideation. Inverse reversal is binary vibrancy and the pulsation that is holographic. Every hologram is a representation of God. This gives God experience through expression. Fear is the isolation of God into specific-ness. Love is the connection of God with Itself, and everything It is not. Love is also the representation of God infinitely.

All that is required is remembering who we are here. There is also letting go of attachment to our body as 'it.' Awareness invites us to familiarize ourselves with the properties of energy and how it works. How it is contributed to others determines the type of service one shares. Do we desire to be wisdom, artistry, and kindness, or are our lives ignorance, brutality, and cruelty? It is left to us to decide and determine where we go from here. For some, it will be what self-destructs. For others, it will be repeating third density elsewhere. For the harvested, it will be the continuation of our species on this planet until it collectively ascends as the Christ. This will be our legacy when love and light are lived as the humanity it is according to the body and spirit. This is what we are learning to be and know humanly. This requires equality and balance to be and know.

Every source that is positive seeks to educate us into love and light as what is real and true that we live as man and woman. Woman is to love what man is to light. We give gender and identity to love and light personally and to its unification into love/light as our self here. Love/light only seeks to increase mass and magnitude as a community of likeminded people. It is not difficult to do, humanly. This only requires people choosing to own love and light and, then, to share these with others without too much ego. Individuality is not as significant as collective states of organization. The ego is a grain of sand when compared with the rest of the self. Connection requires knowing what one is connected to here as an integration. When one can state with certainty, I am God, planet, and universe as a human being according to self and ego, one is ready to ascend, after serving others with a smile.

The heart is the determiner of life lived positively. It is also the residence of God. It connects all of life to every life form and this planet. It is the seat of compassion and kindness. The open heart radiates. The head predisposes us to negativity. It is why we are focused solely on identity, individuality, and negativity. It gives us the idea we are our ego and body only. It is the basis for the biasing of energy into uniqueness. It is the determiner for what is active and what is latent. The positive and negative are balanced as a neutral state. Neutrality seeks to become polarized into path of service. There are those who strive to serve the ego, while some seek to serve others. The rest of us go about our business, oblivious to what human evolution is truly involved with as the ongoing. It is left to each of us to determine what's so and to get involved with that wholeheartedly. There are many voices that claim to know. Only the inner voice matters, as it always speaks that truth needed within one's life to evolve into and through. Many are left guessing, or else deducing ideas into something sensible, yet completely misguided. This is the arbitrary nature of individuality relying solely upon the ego and externals for truth, reality, and the way it is.

Invading the Indigenous while the Rest of Us Watch

The emphasis is always on what unifies, rather than on what destroys or tears down. Unity consciousness is the next level of awareness. This requires letting go of the idea that one is an entity unto him or herself. It is also useful to understand the roles of both the masculine and the feminine as one's life. What is the oneness of diversity? What is the oneness of infinity? These questions are answered by the idea of I Am-ness, as this is the oneness of them, humanly. Our confusion comes from over identifying with the body as an entity unto itself through the ego. The conflict few resolve is between the idea of separation and connection. Separation means life as it is cannot exist. The work is how we reconnect who we are with what is. This unifies God and universe into a synthesis of integrity and wholesomeness. This is coupled with our life as the biology we express on this planet, according to gender and interests.

Everyone agrees to role-play their life for those with whom they are involved. This is as much the purpose of karma as it is interest and experience. This involves specific awareness and holographic consciousness. This allows us to know what universality and the particular are as our life. What does this reality feel like? What does this truth represent? How does our life correspond to the existence of, as it pertains to life and all that is? These questions are left to the reader to answer. Discipline reveals the wisdom needed to answer these questions with clarity and certainty. Confidence comes with applied effort. So does expanded awareness and insight. Ease of being and living are the fruits of our discipline. It is like we give birth to our life as what we become conscious of. Ascension is the birth of what is ongoing as our life and that of what is ascended into. This shows us what we are representing as our life through what we allow ourselves to become the reality of, as our flesh and bones.

We are all shown negatives, positives, and the arbitrary. How we make sense of them and interact with them determines own our evolution. Those who do not get it pass on. The 'awareness of only comes from within. The outer only mirrors back to us what we choose to represent as our life. It can and is anything we feel and think. What we do is what we embody for others to interact within and respond to. Creation arises from a matrix into the potential, acting as a catalyst that we experience. This allows for transformation into greater levels and ways of being and sharing. These showcase our evolution, which is measured by how loving and enlightened we are. Death means we did not get it about life as an extension and expansion of God into everything: God is, the relationship between, and the representation of all that is. This is what mind, body, and spirit are as the humanity we enjoy. This can be thought of as the heart, torso, and head. The heart is God; the torso is the relationship the heart has with itself as the body; and the head is the representation of identity as something specific. All we have to do is know these as oneness. This heals us into wholeness that ascends. This can be thought of as: from the mind; through the body; that the spirit brings to life; and what the soul becomes conscious of, as its own reality, shared as a personal truth. We simply humanize reality and truth into what we live and share. This determines what our life represents. The only difference between our life and that of great teachers is in what they became conscious of, as their reality and truth according to a shared way of living.

Awareness is what we choose to focus on. What we give importance to determines where we place our attention and what we give enough meaning to, in order to allow our life to experience that, so we can be and know what the experience is as our life. This will involve positives, negatives, and the arbitrary. A given life can be whatever is desired. What is, is represented as our life. Then, we get to feel what our life is as that. Change is inevitable. This is the art of fine- tuning our life into what we feel best represents our ideal. When a given catalyst is no longer needed, our life will change into other states of being. Death is such an end. Anytime something is lost, we are given the opportunity of growth and wisdom. Resistance only means instant replay until we get it. Reincarnation only means we have not gotten it about living life as a human being. We keep coming back until reality and truth are owned and lived humanly, then we evolve beyond the human condition into greater levels of

Invading the Indigenous while the Rest of Us Watch

being based upon love, light, and consciousness. We are here to remember the nature of the self through serving others.

People live exactly as their life is designed to, according to the soul's blueprint. There is only perfection with this, according to what is intended. Humanly, life comes down to issues needing healing and the development of talents into what is shared through joy. Coupled with this is expanded awareness. These can be thought of as the physical and the spiritual. There is also the mind and soul to become conscious of. This is only done when one seeks to become conscious of them and what they pertain to, humanly. Often we are fooled by false doctrine. It can lead us astray for as long as we are enticed by that. When going within, most erroneous ideas fade away, along with those people who insist their life is that. By doing so, these people show us what we have outgrown, humanly. Outgrowing, or evolving beyond the human condition, is ascension. In its truest form, the body is taken with one when one leaves. Death of the body and reincarnation of the soul are the same experience. Death means one did not get it.

What does it take for us to become conscious? It depends on what our issues are and why we are here. This will differ from person to person. Also, what does it take for us to get along and be friendly? Seems very odd to me that I can count on my two hands all the people I consider friends. Only shows me how unfriendly we are in this day and age. A shame we have not evolved beyond limitations and the invader culture mindset. Negativity as our individuality is ending as death and destruction. Those who refuse to end these as their psychology will experience these as the end of their world here forever. Extinction shows us our refusal to evolve beyond what is untenable as our life. The end times only involve that which is no longer relevant or pertaining to this planet and our human beingness. Those who are not harvested will repeat hiser experience elsewhere. Anyone who has not resolved fear as a catalyst will become extinct. What survive humanly are only those people whose lives involve and pertain to the new reality. As it stands now, it is less than one percent of humanity.

Douglas H. Melloy

Individuality is ending as a predominant, humanly. Humanity is evolving into a collective state of socialism. There is only the family of humanity existing as the Christ when love and light are lived consciously. Lacking these as one's life means death is assured. Death is a choice. Life is a choice. One either lives or dies. Life requires living, the inclusion of God, affirmation of life, and involvement with humanness. Death is the exclusion of God as it is humanly, the negation of life, and aversion to what makes us the image and likeness of God. People must truly desire to be what is real as a personal truth before their life becomes that. This will be a consternation to everyone who lives what fades away. One will only lose what they never owned. This includes life.

Arbitrariness is a curious way some people choose to exist. Nothing matters beyond addictions, distractions, and dysfunctions. Beliefs that are meaningless and irrelevant are considered to be real, true, and the way it is. Many never question why they believe what they do, so they remain ignorant about reality and truth as it involves and pertains to our design. Arbitrariness has its usefulness in that it allows people personal choices and unique ways of being. Why someone has hiser likes and dislikes is strictly personal and arbitrary. We are entitled to live exactly as we choose. It is our divine right and the way free will works. Conformity is a form of insanity. Nothing is like anything else. Uniqueness is infinity, which is non-repetition, so why do so many involve themselves in ideologies that have nothing to do with their true identities? "I am a Hindu, a Buddhist, a Muslim, or a Christian" means God is not allowed Its humanness. Neither are life, identity, the universe; but then, that is the role religion plays for those who place their faith in theologies that only teach false doctrine about God, life, humanness, and all that is resulting in the death experience.

The body is only a holographic projection of the mind. It represents God on this planet humanly. It is the objectification of God in human form. The ego is the mask the body wears giving specific-ness to experiences that correspond to what it embodies for the evolution of the soul. Evolution is the only relevance of

Invading the Indigenous while the Rest of Us Watch

existence. What evolves is consciousness through experience that is involved with itself and others, either positively or negatively. People are attracted to what they feel represents them. This is the arbitrariness of experience. It is only reality and truth that matters as our evolution. Everything else is just an aspect of imagination. It is our make believe. According to Conversations With God, "We are making this all up as we go."

To truly live humanly and positively, people must be heart centered. It is here our connection with all else exists. When people are involved with a common interest, it is the heart that connects them to each other. The energy of the heart connects with those who are also involved. The common denominator for all of us is our human being-ness. This establishes connected integration between people of like mind. Humanity now is out of sync with others, the planet, God, and universe. These states of existence are treated like they are foreign to us and not who we are; we wonder why we feel so alien to this planet and each other. Isolationism rules our lives. Everything is treated at a distance, so the reality of, as a personal truth, is never known and owned.

People holding to fear will attach themselves to ideologies that they feel protect them from what they are afraid of as an external, like books or people considered knowledgeable. Usually, what we believe in reinforces what we feel is our reality and the way it is here. Billions believe in the ideas of good versus evil, sin, fallenness, hell, and the social practices of war, greed, class distinction, and slavery. These have colored the history of this planet. What about her story? It is left unsaid and unwritten. It is ignored. Love has all but disappeared as an active state as the physical embodiment we are living.

We live in our heads, not our hearts, so the death experience is inevitable. We currently live in a country with billionaires and those living on the street. This disparity alone shows us how out of sync we are with our own humanity. What we see is a total lack of equality and balance, humanly. The greater the level of inequality and imbalance lived, the greater the magnitude of earth changes needed to correct them. This is what humanity faces within the next few years. The planet will heal itself of our negativity. It will do so through heat and salt. These are how a planet heals itself of all the negativity embedded in it surface, going back thousands of years. Most of humanity is oblivious to this currently. The end times mentioned by so many only involve negativity as our individual biasing. It is the ending of fear as our ways of death, destruction, and disaster. Oneness, healing, and wholeness will return to our way of being and living not without a struggle by those who serve themselves, and by those sources with an investment in negative socialisms. The games as played involve fear, judgment, and persecution, personally; and war, greed, and class distinction, socially. All involved with these will discover their world has come to an end forever as far as this planet is concerned, for there is no coming back here. This involves most of humanity.

    Human evolution is measured by what is healed. Almost everything that has afflicted those of the past afflicts us now. It is like we have not evolved in eleven thousand years. Many nonphysical beings do not understand why we have not evolved. They wonder why we are so addicted and attached to what kills us. They wonder why war and greed are still important to us, given they are insignificant. They wonder why we are so indifferent to each other and the beauty of this planet. They wonder why death is more important to us than life itself. Why fear is more real to us than love.

    History is recorded by all the wars fought. Obviously, war is considered more important than any other social activity. The question is why? It is what we place our faith in, religiously. The days of war are coming to an end. Third density is ending. A new earth is coming into existence. Only those whose lives are the new reality will be here to evolve our species into what is eternal in nature and design. Most of humanity will not make the transition, due to not focusing on what the nature of the self' is and how this evolves through experience into the universal. Move away from places where there are large numbers of people. Mass consciousness acts like a blanket, covering people with what is believed by those

Invading the Indigenous while the Rest of Us Watch

congregating together in numbers exceeding two thousand people. This involves most cities and towns. Living at higher elevations is also wise. The days of transition will be like a hiccup. When the dust settles, we will look around and smile, glad to be alive and in one piece.

The idea of what ends only makes sense when we know what does and why. Life is created to give God specific experiences in and with I Am-ness. Evolution prior to the human required birth and death to take place. This is not the case with our design. It has the potential of ascending, but only when love and light are owned, lived, and shared with others joyously and happily. The invader culture will become extinct very soon. Humanity will return to living as designed. For most of humanity, it is time for the soul to return to where it has come from. The work in personality is finished. Now, it is time for humanity to become the Christ it is, so that this will ascend as the one being that is collective ascension.

Douglas H. Melloy

Conclusion

    The art of propaganda is how well it fools humanity through those institutions designed to do this. There are seven right now: science, religion, education, business, politics, medicine, and law. These keep us steeped in what soon becomes extinct--the invader culture mindset. The book of Revelation and the Mayan Calendar tell us why and when. Humanity has turned a blind eye to what is now obvious. God, life, humanness, and service are what evolve as us. These are what we exist as, humanly. This requires our choosing to become conscious of them as our life, as well as to why we are here and what we are becoming, which is the Christ consciousness that collectively ascends when people live love and light consciously for each other.

    According to the RA Material, third density ends and fourth density begins. What this means for all of us is: that which exists contrary to our design will end, becoming extinct, for it is our true nature that evolves, which is positive as love and light. Living as designed is living indigenously. This will evolve us until we collectively ascend. The irony is, humanity has missed the point of what is going on and why. This involves only service polarity as the 'wheat' of our species. The chaff is made up of those souls who live arbitrarily by not addressing and owning what evolves and why. There are individual sources, like the ascended masters, who communicate to us. There are other self-polarized entities that disseminate propaganda to disempower us in order to empower themselves. Then, there are collective states of being that share information with us.

    We are attracted to those sources that match and mirror our own point of view. Individuality does not actually exist only collective states do. People are stuck and live like particles in a state

Invading the Indigenous while the Rest of Us Watch

of chaos. Few have evolved their way of being from the particle, beyond the wave, and into what is holographic in nature and design, so they miss the point entirely of what it is and means to be human. Death is missing the point.

Negativity as a predominator ends very soon. What causes the extinction of that will take all those who are involved with that way of life. Those who live arbitrarily will find that they become unviable as well. Only those who are living as designed will survive. This is about 0.7 percent of humanity. That means 99,3 percent of humanity will not survive! All because they choose to live what does not actually exist as our humanness. The timeline is the end of 2012. Humanity is returning to living the Christ as a collective state that will ascend--but not before the invader culture mindset becomes extinct and those who live small mindedly go home.

It is always our choice as to what we feel and think as the ideologies we engage in, humanly. Many are seduced by the ideas of the self-serving, which make the invader culture viable and ongoing, until it becomes extinct. Conquering, enslaving, and destroying are not understood. Death is this on a personal level. Living life is owning and sharing will, love, light, and consciousness, as they exist humanly. Humanity has decided to be the intentions of things external, fear, darkness, and unconsciousness, which are our life and legacy. This is flatly not true, so what humanity faces is the end of the road for everyone not living who they are as designed.

The invader culture mindset soon becomes extinct. Those living arbitrarily soon go home. Those living as designed consciously return our ideal to existing with and in accordance to nature as the planetary ideal we are, humanly. False doctrines end, and just like the dinosaurs became unviable here, so will those who refuse to live as we are created to exist, humanly. We have been given more than enough time to accomplish this. It is up to each of us to choose what we wish to be, know, share, and ascend. Selfishness is the great fiction, as is war, greed, and class distinction. Within a medium that is infinite-the universe--nothing has greater or lesser value than anything else. A grain of sand has as much value as an entire galaxy.

Douglas H. Melloy

It is only the foolish and deceived that live thinking they are superior to others, like the warlord god Jehovah.

There are no excuses for what is obvious to us when we are humble enough to see what is shown to us, which is the equality and balance of the reality and truth we humanize. Reality, as a personal truth, always evolves into a greater level of self- awareness beyond ideologies that are misguided and confused to the death. Evolution takes no prisoners! It evolves beyond the figments of those who only care about self-interested gains of self-destruction, fueled by the pursuits of war, greed, and class distinction. These are the follies of the confused. Stillness, peace, and harmony are life as the planet and all of its life forms, which shows us God's infinitude.

There is only the oneness of God as all that is. Those conflicted within seek to destroy God, so they subscribe to ideologies that allow for war and death to exist as a personal way of life. This is not our design. Good versus evil, holy war, and survival of the fittest are false ideas disseminated to lead us to the grave. They are taught intentionally to confuse us. Out of the infinite possibilities that exist, we choose many that are very un-evolved and death inducing. The illusions stand in order that we can believe what we want to. It is our divine right to do so. It is only in going it alone that one discovers what is according to hiser life. Then, one gets to share that with others humbly and transparently.

The world 'ends' because those who do not survive will leave convinced it has, as there is no coming back here for those who do not remain to continue the evolution of our species. This means the birth, crucifixion, death, and reincarnation cycles end for souls and this planet. Evolution will have to continue on another planet similar to this one. Does another one like this exist? I was told that there is not one now, and that it will be ten million years before the conditions exist for another planet of this nature to exist.

Even when life is shown to us, we still choose death and selfishness to behaviorize. Even when love and light are observed as the sun, we choose fear and darkness. Even when we see others, we only care about our whims of the moment. People spend their

Invading the Indigenous while the Rest of Us Watch

entire lives conforming to ideals that soon become extinct. We refuse to see others as ourselves, so we miss what the Christ is, as humanity living what is conducive and ongoing. We think heaven is where we go after we have died. Heaven is here when one lives what this is now.

The ending of the invader culture mindset happens when the warlord god Jehovah returns for Its chosen people and for those who engage and support that way of selfishness. Those who live arbitrarily, it's time for you to go home as well, for you are not contributing to the social evolution of our design. Indigenous people exist for a reason. They are how we were created to exist humanly, according to the love of Yahweh and light of Id. These two beings are our creator and bestower gods. They are why 'our' is referenced in the Bible in the first chapter of Genesis.

People are fooled by external sources due to their refusal to trust their own intuition, which is how the soul communicates to us. Most of humanity relies only on what the five senses observe and on what others claim is the way it is. The expectation placed upon us is to believe what we are told by 'experts' that are clueless. This is especially true when it comes to science and religion. People live as if their ego is 'it' in all contexts and capacities.

We will see the extinction of the invader culture mindset very soon, possibly as early as the end of 2012. Humanness is designed to live indigenously, which is what we will return to living as. To those who live arbitrarily, it is time for you to go home. Look to the skies, as that is why UFOs are here; they are here to take your soul back to where it came from. The good news is, we get to choose what we live as, humanly. It is either as someone negative, positive, or arbitrary.

Douglas H. Melloy

Aware Talk Radio

Join Us - LIVE - 7 Nights A Week!!!
Or Listen To Past Archives:
www.innercirclepublishing.com
http://www.blogtalkradio.com/aware

Call In Number: (646) 716-8138

Aware Talk Radio incorporates all fields of science, from the normal to the paranormal, from the physical to the metaphysical. We seek to expand the awareness of humankind. Your Comments, Questions, and Guest Suggestions are welcome.

Invading the Indigenous while the Rest of Us Watch

www.ingramcontent.com/pod-product-compliance
Lightning Source LLC
Chambersburg PA
CBHW060827050426
42453CB00008B/609